The Worship
of the Lord Jesus Christ
in the Old Testament

Gerard De Gols (1676-1737)

Edited
by Douglas Van Dorn

The Worship
of the Lord Jesus Christ
in the Old Testament

Gerard De Gols (1676-1737)

Edited
by Douglas Van Dorn

Waters of Creation Publishing
Dacono, Colorado

ISBN-13:978-0-9862376-7-6 (Waters of Creation Publishing)

Contents

Other Books by Waters of Creation

Waters of Creation: A Biblical-Theological Study of Baptism (2009)
Galatians: A Supernatural Justification (2012)
Giants: Sons of the Gods (2013)
Covenant Theology: A Reformed Baptist Primer (2014)
From the Shadows to the Savior: Christ in the Old Testament (2015)
The Unseen Realm: Q & A Companion (2016)
Five Solas (2019)

Christ in All Scripture Series

Vol. 1. *Appearances of the Son of God Under the Old Testament* by John Owen (2019)

Vol. 2. *A Dissertation Concerning the Angel who is called the Redeemer and Other Select Passages* by Peter Allix (2020)

Vol. 3. *The Worship of the Lord Jesus Christ in the Old Testament* by Gerard De Gols (2020)

Vol. 4. *The Angel of the LORD In Early Jewish, Christian, and Reformation History,* a compilation of Allix, Owen, and De Gols (2020)

Vol. 5. *Christ in the Old Testament: Promised, Patterned, and Present* revised and expanded second edition of the previously titled: *From the Shadows to the Savior: Christ in the Old Testament* by Douglas Van Dorn (2020).

Vol. 6. *Jesus: Who, What, Where, When, Why?* by Douglas Van Dorn (2020)

For more information, articles, radio shows, and broadcasts go to: dougvandorn.com

Editor's Introduction

Reason for This Series

I am convinced, after studying the topic of Christ in the Old Testament in some depth for the last several years, and having lived in modern conservative Reformed and Evangelical Christian circles for nearly 50 years, that too many Christians (past and present) far too often presuppose and/or superimpose a kind of Unitarian grid upon the OT. This is a very Liberal way of reading the Scripture, out of line with orthodox Christian teaching throughout history.

It isn't that this is done malevolently, for these same Christians often do see Christ in the OT in one way or another. I am not talking about a Christianity that outright denies the deity of Jesus. In fact, I'm talking about a Christianity that loves him as the *Theanthropos*—The God-man. It isn't that this is done deliberately either. At least, not usually. I would say it is more of a subconscious decision. We speak about Christ being there in type and shadow, but to say that he was actually there—*in person?* This is a hard pill for many to swallow. I had more than one professor in my conservative Baptist schooling tell the students that to see Christ or a Trinity actually there, as if any of the human authors could have deliberately written about these things when they wrote the OT books, was reading the NT back into the Old. It was eisegesis, not exegesis.

In this way, too many of us presuppose that the Jewish Church did not, indeed *could not* have known the Christ to write about him actually being present in their midst. He simply wasn't there among them. At best, only the Father was. Yet, somehow, we think, they could foresee his coming. But this is a strange oxymoron, because that would seem to itself presuppose that they knew he already existed, if the Messiah they prophesied about was truly God. But if they knew he already existed, why couldn't he have known them or made himself know to them? Nevertheless, at the end of the day when we ask questions like *Job knew his Redeemer* (Job 19:25) *to be Christ?* Or *Solomon comprehended the Son of a Father who has ascended to heaven* (Prov 30:4) *was Christ?* Or *Abraham believed God* (Gen 15:6), *whom he knew to be Christ?* Not possible is a very common answer to hear.

As a case in point, there is an ancient manuscript variant in Jude 5 where one family of texts say "Jesus" lead Israel in the Exodus, while another family reads the "Lord" did it. Apparently, this discussion has been around for a long, long time. Some scribe was asking the same question: *Jude could call the Savior of the Exodus "Jesus?"* Not possible. So he changed "Jesus" to "Lord." The renowned NT scholar Bruce Metzger ran into the same skepticism I have run into in conservative circles on this very same variant when he was working on his *Textual Commentary on the Greek New Testament* in a committee with a bunch of other scholars. He wrote, "A majority of the Committee was of the opinion that the [Jesus] reading was difficult to the point of impossibility."[1]

Why? Because we presuppose it, that's why. Therefore, any OT text you can think of where a Christian has argued that we see the Trinity or Christ ("Holy, Holy, Holy" or "Let us make man in our image") must be dismissed out of hand.

The Place of this Work in This Series

The work before you is a volume in the Series: Christ in the Old Testament, by Waters of Creation Publishing. At present, this series consists of the following volumes:

---

[1] Bruce Manning Metzger, United Bible Societies, *A Textual Commentary on the Greek New Testament, Second Edition a Companion Volume to the United Bible Societies' Greek New Testament (4th Rev. Ed.)* (London; New York: United Bible Societies, 1994), 657.

- *A Dissertation Concerning the Angel who is called the Redeemer and Other Select Passages* by Peter Allix
- *Appearances of the Son of God Under the Old Testament* by John Owen
- *The Worship of the Lord Jesus Christ in the Old Testament* by Gerard De Gols
- *The Angel of the LORD In Early Jewish, Christian, and Reformation History*, a compilation of Allix, Owen, and De Gols
- *Christ in the Old Testament: Promised, Patterned, and Present* by Douglas Van Dorn
- *Jesus: Who, What, Where, When, Why?* by Douglas Van Dorn

This book serves as either a supplement or stand-alone book. As a supplement, it belongs with the forthcoming book by Matt Foreman and Douglas Van Dorn on the Angel of the LORD. Matt and I were simply not able to put all the material in that volume that we wanted, and the present book fills a needed gap.

Before you now is a significant portion of a powerful, persuasive, and pastoral work titled (in good Puritanical tradition), *A Vindication of the worship of the Lord Jesus Christ as the Supreme God, in all the dispensations, patriarchal, mosaick and Christian : demonstrating, that Christ was so known and worship'd in all ages, from Adam to this day*, by Gerard De Gols.

The book was is written to Peter Lord King (1669-1734), cousin of John Locke and Baron of Ockham who became Lord High Chancellor of Great

Britain, although it is clear that De Gols did not know King, but did reply that unlike his cousin, King "understands the matters" and "believes the Scripture" which is "the great honor of any magistrate to therefore honor and adore God before me." He begins the work with over 120 contemporary names that are all in agreement with its contents. What we will concern ourselves with is the 5th-9th chapters.

We begin at De Gol's unfolding the divinity of Christ in many parallel texts with his Father. He looks especially at the incommunicable attributes of God, which God and God alone can have. Yet, Christ has them too. This lengthy chapter, which can be challenging to read especially at the beginning, is nevertheless of powerful apologetic value for anyone seeking to defend the deity of Christ and his oneness with the Father against skeptics or cults. In this, it also serves as a tool to strengthen one's own faith.

This then lays the foundation for seeing Christ worshiped throughout the OT as the Angel of the LORD, the Memra, Word, or Logos with a special attention given to a great many OT saints (Adam, Cain and Abel, Enoch, Noah, Melchizedek, Abraham, Hagar, Lot, Isaac, Jacob, Joseph, Moses, Job, Israel in the wilderness, Joshua, Gideon, Manoah, the prophets, David, Solomon, and more) whom De Gols powerfully demonstrates "worshiped Christ as God." This latter section is highly valuable for pastoral care, especially as it relates to helping people see that yes, indeed, those in the OT explicitly knew and worshiped Jesus Christ.

It is almost completely unheard of today that anyone would be so bold as to say that the saints of the OT worshiped Christ as God. Thus, I cannot recommend De Gols highly enough for anyone struggling with or knows someone who struggles with the deity of Christ, for it is his deity, his eternality that allows him to even be present in OT times in order to be worshiped. It is one of the greatest books I can imagine being written to confirm our trust that the New Testament authors knew what they were talking about when they, in every single chapter, returned to the Old Testament to demonstrate the divinity of Jesus Christ. De Gols wants you to believe that Jesus was there, present in the OT, known, and worshiped by all the OT saints. For anyone who desires to have a better grasp of these things, this is the book for you.

Gerard De Gols

The work and its author are virtually unknown. Perhaps this is due in part because very little is known about Gerard De Gols. He was born in Amsterdam around 1676. His father's name was Philip. He was admitted to the Trinity College at Cambridge at the age of 17 in 1693 and two years later he was admitted to the school of St. Paul's. At some point he seems to have gone to Leyden to study in the Netherlands. De Gols became the Rector of St. Peter's Anglican church in Sandwich, England where he presided for 24 years (1713-37), though one source says he began his work here in 1706. He was also a minister to the Dutch congregation at St. Clement's in Sandwich. One of the only remaining facts that we know about him is that he was so well respected by his fellow-townsmen that he was one of the persons selected by the corporation to support the canopies at the coronation of George II and Queen Caroline. He wrote and published *Sermons* (1711-26), a poem called *Samson, or the Unhappy Lover* (London, 1696), as well as the present book which was published in London in 1726. He died on Feb. 22, 1737 at the age of 61 and is buried at St. Clement's.

A Note on Editing

I have updated antiquated terms and phrases. In many cases, I have used the ESV for the biblical citation, though any time I felt the original (often the KJV or Geneva Bible) made the point more strongly, I have retained it or made my own translation as close to the original, but with modern language, as I could.

Whenever I could find a modern English translation of a work in a footnote, I have changed the citations to fit the modern English text. In other cases, I have left the citation and its reference unchanged. It is up to the reader to track those down. Many of the

Scripture passages quoted were originally italicized. I have retained this and italicized the Targum quotations as well. Capitalization was a bit of a subjective decision. Old English capitalized many more words than we do. If I felt a word in any way applied to an attribute or name of God, it remains capitalized, though sometimes this may seem inconsistent because of the context.

My hope is that being confronted by De Gols and the myriad of Jews and Church Fathers he cites will help settle the reader into a sure and certain confidence as to the much questioned fact that the OT church did in fact know and worship the Lord Jesus Christ, especially when he came to them as the Angel of the LORD, who is, in fact, the Second Person of the Holy Trinity, the Son pre-incarnate, the Redeemer whom those people before Messiah came knew, trusted in, and worshiped as Yahweh-God.

A more important topic is difficult to discern, especially in days like ours when the Old Testament has fallen on such hard times. Reading others who have gone before us talk about Him in such clear, profound, and direct ways should be a balm to the soul of any Christian and a powerful apologetic against unbelief.

Doug Van Dorn
January 2020

——— ——— ———

Excerpts from:
A Vindication of the Worship of the Lord Jesus Christ as the Supreme God

By
Gerard De Gols

CHAP. V.

THAT DIVINE ADORATION IS DUE TO CHRIST, BECAUSE HE IS GOD.

We come now to demonstrate that this holy worship, this divine adoration, which is God's due and his incommunicable attributes, are applied to the Lord Christ in the Scriptures and required of us to be paid to Christ by the Scriptures. This I shall demonstrate, by showing that Christ is that God who is to be worshiped.

We Christians profess that there is one and only one God. This is the fundamental article of all religion. And we believe that this God, whose highest perfection is that he cannot lie, can no more deceive us than he can be deceived by us. We believe that this God is one only, and that in the unity of that divinity there are three Persons: the Father, the Son, and the Holy Ghost who are that one God. This we believe although we cannot understand it, because that great God, who alone knows himself, has to reveal himself to us. Yet, we are assured that this great God is too holy to deceive us, too good to lead us into error, and too jealous of his honor to make anyone else who is not God a sharer of his prerogatives or a partaker of his worship and adoration.

Thus, we find ourselves obliged to believe this Trinity of Persons in the unity of the divinity from most express words of Scripture. For those sacred pages assure us both in the Old and New Testament:

That there is but One True God.

In the Old Testament	In the New Testament
Deut 6:4. *Hear Israel, the Lord our God is one Lord.*	Mark 12:29. *And Jesus answered him— "Hear O Israel, the Lord our God is one Lord."*
Isaiah 46:8. *Is there a God besides me? There is no Rock; I know not any.*	1Co 8:4. *There is no God but One.*
	Gal 3:20. *God is one.*

The same holy pages assure us, both in the Old and New Testament:

That there are Three Persons in the Unity of the Divinity, the Father, Son, and Holy Spirit.

In the Old Testament	In the New Testament
Gen 1:26. *Let us make man in our image, after our Likeness.*[2] Ps 33:6. *By the Word of the LORD the heavens were made, and by the Breath [Spirit] of his mouth all their host.* Ps 45:6. *Your throne, O God, is forever and ever. The scepter of your kingdom is a scepter of uprightness … God, your God has anointed you.*	Matt 3:16-17. *And behold, the heavens were opened to him, and he saw the Spirit of God descending like a dove and coming to rest on him; and behold, a voice from heaven said, "This is my beloved Son, in whom I am well pleased."* Matt 28:19. *Go therefore and make disciples of all nations, baptizing them in the name of the Father and of the Son and of the Holy Spirit.*

---

[2] Original note: "God speaking in the plural number ["us"] here expresses a plurality of Persons in the unity of the divinity; for that God spoke not to the angels is certain, because they had no hand in the creation, neither was man made after their image, but only God's: And that God did not speak in the plural number after the manner of princes, is as certain, because it is evident that the eastern princes spoke in the singular (Dan 4:4, 18, 20; 5:14; 6:26). And God always spoke by the prophets in the singular number (Gen 17:1; Ex 20:2; Num 14:35; and elsewhere)." Editor's note. Many scholars have questioned this assumption that God did not speak to angels (i.e. in the divine council) here. However, even if they are correct and God is here addressing the divine council, we find all three Persons associated with the council elsewhere in Scripture, they are all three clearly in Genesis 1:1-3, and therefore the point of this being a proof-text for the three Persons is still valid.

Ps 110:1. *The LORD said to my Lord.*

Isa 61:1. *The Spirit of the Lord GOD is upon me, because the LORD has anointed.*

Isa 63:9,10, 11, 14. *The Angel of his Presence saved them ... but they rebelled and grieved his Holy Spirit ... The Spirit of the LORD gave them rest.*

[Num 6:24, 25, 26. Isa 6:3, 8; 33:22].

John 10:30. *I am my Father are One.*

John 14:17. *I will ask the Father, and He will give you another Helper ... even the Spirit of Truth.*

2Co 13:14. *The Grace of the Lord Jesus Christ and the love of God and the fellowship of the Holy Spirit be with you all.*

1Jn 5:7. *For there are three that bear record in heaven, the Father, the Word, and the Holy Ghost: and these three are one.*[3]

The same holy Scriptures tell us both in the Old and New Testament:

---

[3] The original note here is an apologetic for the authenticity of these words in the original manuscript. He cites one "Mr. Whiston" who "imposes a most horrid falsehood upon the world, in asserting that this verse never was in the text until about the middle of the reign of Queen Elizabeth, and that no Greek copy in the world that was really written before printing ever had it otherwise than in the margin." De Gols is quite certain that it is found all the way back to the second century. Modern scholarship has shown that these words were in fact a later addition. Metzger explains that no Greek Fathers ever quoted it; it is absent in all ancient versions of the Syriac, Coptic, Armenian, Ethiopic, Arabic, and Slavonic texts. It appears to have been a marginal note that was added because the copiest interpreted the original text to symbolize the Trinity. This then made its way into one line of Latin texts. It doesn't really matter, because there are plenty of other passages that clearly show three Persons sharing one divine Nature. See Bruce Manning Metzger, United Bible Societies, *A Textual Commentary on the Greek New Testament, Second Edition a Companion Volume to the United Bible Societies' Greek New Testament (4th Rev. Ed.)* (London; New York: United Bible Societies, 1994), 647-48.

That this God is holy and just,
that he cannot lie nor deceive us.

In the Old Testament

Ps 89:35. *Once for all I have sworn by my holiness; I will not lie.*

In the New Testament

Tit 1:2. *God, who never lies.* Heb 6:18. *It is impossible for God to lie.*

And lastly, the same Scriptures assure us, both in the Old and New Testament:

That God will not give his Honor to any created Being.

In the Old Testament

Isa 42:8. *I am the LORD; that is my Name; my Glory I give to no other.*

In the New Testament

Php 2:10. *That at the Name of Jesus every knee should bow.* Jude 25. *To the only wise God, our Savior, through Jesus Christ our Lord, be Glory, Majesty, Dominion, and Power, both now and forever. Amen.*

Having therefore this foundation of God's veracity and concern for his own honor, and he having so plainly revealed to us that there are three Persons in the unity of the divine majesty, we humbly receive his revelation with all due regard and most awful [profoundly reverential] submission. And this we believe, although we do not have a full perception of it. We believe it on the authority and fidelity of the most holy God who has revealed it, although we do not understand how that can be. We are not desirous of searching into that secret which God has withheld from us, and reserved for a brighter light, and a more exalted station. We are satisfied it is so, though we do not know how.

Even with respect to the creation, we believe the creatures are made, though we do not understand how they were made. We jangle not with the works of God, because we do not know how he made them; for it is my opinion that if we perfectly understood how any of the creatures were made, we should be able to make them too. Since we are therefore satisfied about the one, why should we not be about the other? For if we do not know the architecture of a fly, nor understand the formation of a gnat, which surpasses our understanding as much as our power to make them, how much more unable are we to comprehend the nature of that Being, who infinitely exceeds all beings, the Lord and giver of life?

In confidence therefore of God's truthfulness, and in reliance on his wisdom, holiness, and truth, we believe that there are three Persons in the undivided unity of the divinity; and that Jesus Christ, whom we, and all the host of heaven, and all the churches on earth adore, is the true God. We adore him as God with the same honor and worship as we honor the Father, and that not rashly, not unadvisedly, not inconsiderately, but according to and in obedience to God's own command, "*That all may honor the Son, just as they honor the Father. Whoever does not honor the Son does not honor the Father who sent him*" (John 5:22, 23). These words most positively instruct that the very same honor must be paid to the Son as is paid to the Father, and that whatever pretense men may make, that honor is due to the Father only, that God here himself testifies that he is dishonored if the same honor that is due to him is not paid to the Son. The reason and foundation is because this Son, this Jesus Christ, is very God—is really and truly God.

That Christ is that very God that is to be worshiped, appears:

From the Divine Names.

All the names and titles which belong to the glorious majesty of God are given to the Lord Christ; and these are not given once, but always; not only without, but with the distinguishing article; not barely, but with the most glorious attributes in the very same manner as they are given to God the Father. He is called God absolutely, the incommunicable Name of *JEHOVAH* [YHWH] is given to him. He is called the true God, the mighty God, the great God and Saviour. All the sublime titles whereby the only true God is dignified and distinguished are given to him.

Jesus Christ is Jehovah God.

The Jews say that *JEHOVAH* is God's proper name, and so peculiarly God's name, that it never was nor can be communicated to any created being.[4] And this is grounded upon the Scriptures: Isa 42:8, "*I am the Lord [Jehovah], that is my Name; my Glory I give to no other, nor my praise to carved idols;*" and Hosea 12:5, "*The LORD God of Hosts, the LORD is his memorial Name,*" where the word "*memorial*" excludes all created beings from participating in that name, and appropriates it to God alone. God himself insists upon his being Jehovah alone, in opposition to all other gods, glorying, in a manner, and triumphing in it as the distinguishing character by which he would be known to be infinitely superior to all the gods of the nations. Ex 12:12, "*On all the Gods of Egypt I will execute judgments, I am the LORD (Jehovah);*" Jer 32:27, "*I am the LORD (Jehovah), the God of all flesh. Is there anything too hard for me?*"

The Jews further say[5] that in the letters of the name Jehovah, the three tenses (past, present, and future) are contained: was, is, and shall be. We add that St. John from this interprets it, "*Who is, who was, and*

---

[4] De Gols cites Boxtorf. *Lexicon Hebraicum* (1607), p. 157 here. This refers to Johannes Buxtorf (1564-1629), a Hebraist and professor of Hebrew for thirty-nine years at Basel. He was known as the "Master of the Rabbis."

[5] Buxtorf, Ibid.

is to come" (Rev 1:18). Thus, it is called the name of God's existence; for when God had said, "*I AM WHAT I AM*" (Ex 3:14), he then immediately calls himself *JEHOVAH* (vs. 15), and he says that this is his peculiar name. "*This is my Name for ever, and this is my Memorial unto all Generations.*" Our adversaries [the Socinians][6] do allow that the name Jehovah has reference to the necessary existence of the Person so named in his own right.[7]

And this name JEHOVAH, this peculiar name, which the Psalmist says is God's name alone (Ps 83:18) is given to the Son of God, even to Jesus Christ. This name is distinguished in our translation by capital letters, though the word *Jah*, which is a contraction of Jehovah, is noted with the same capitals and also rendered LORD.[8]

In the Old Testament

Isa 45:21-25. *There is no other god besides me, a righteous God and a Savior; there is none besides me. Turn to me and be saved, all the ends of the earth! For I am*

In the New Testament

Rom 14:10-11. *For we will all stand before the judgment seat of God; for it is written, "As I live, says the Lord, every knee shall bow to*

---

[6] Named for Italian theologian Fausto Sozzini (Lat: Faustus Socinus). Socinianism is nontrinitarian in its view of Christ and precursor to many forms of Unitarianism within Protestantism.

[7] Original note: Clarke's *Reply*, p. 164. Editor's note. This is Samuel Clarke (1675-1729), a Socinian and anti-Trinitarian leader of the Enlightenment. He believed that Christ was merely a man.

[8] Original note: Ex 15:2; 17:16; in the Psalms often; Isa 38:11; Song of Solomon 8:6.

God, and there is no other. By myself I have sworn; from my mouth has gone out in righteousness a word that shall not return: "To me every knee shall bow, every tongue shall swear allegiance." Only in the LORD, it shall be said of me, are righteousness and strength; to him shall come and be ashamed all who were incensed against him. In the LORD all the offspring of Israel shall be justified and shall glory. Isa 44:6. *Thus says the LORD, the King of Israel and his Redeemer, the LORD of hosts: "I am the first and I am the last; besides me there is no god."*

me, and every tongue shall confess to God." Php 2:9-11. *Therefore God has highly exalted him and bestowed on him the name that is above every name, so that at the name of Jesus every knee should bow, in heaven and on earth and under the earth, and every tongue confess that Jesus Christ is Lord, to the glory of God the Father.* Rev 1:8. *"I am the Alpha and the Omega," says the Lord God, "who is and who was and who is to come, the Almighty."*

It would never end if we enumerated all the texts of Scripture, for it is observed that the name Jehovah is more than sixty times given to Christ in the Old Testament, and all such places, as by the authority of Christ and the Apostles, are applied to Christ in the New Testament, as the Son of God and the Savior of the world. I shall only take notice of one more.

In the Old Testament
Jer 23:6. *In his days Judah will be saved, and Israel will dwell securely. And this is the name by*

In the New Testament
1Co 1:30. *And because of him you are in Christ Jesus, who became to us wisdom from*

> *which he will be called: "The*   *God, righteousness and sanc-*
> *LORD is our righteousness."*   *tification and redemption.*

Here, I observe that the *"Lord our Righteousness"* is not all the name of Christ, but Jehovah alone; and *"our Righteousness"* is a description both of his divine nature, and of the mercy mankind should receive from him. In the original it is *tzidkenu* ("righteousness") and Buxtorf tells us that the word *tsedeq* ("righteous") was a common addition to the titles of the kings of Jerusalem.[9] And so here Christ is called *"Jehovah the righteous,"* and particularly *"our Righteousness,"* to declare his government and what mankind should receive from him, who is both their King and their God. This text is explained by Jer 33:16 where it is not said to be his name, but his title, and description of his nature.

I shall only add, that the Jews say[10] the name Jehovah is not only God's great and glorious name, but that it is also the name of grace and mercy from Exodus 34:6. *"The LORD, the LORD, a God merciful and gracious, slow to anger, and abounding in steadfast love and faithfulness."* That this name of grace belongs to the Messiah, the same Jews acknowledge when they say, "Why do the Israelites pray, and are not heard? The answer is because they do not understand (*Shemhamphorash*) the name of Jehovah explained, but in the age

---

[9] Buxtorf, *Lex.* 638.
[10] Ibid., 30 & 167.

of the Messiah God shall make it known to them, and then shall they be heard."

And again, "The Scripture says, the name of the Messiah is the LORD OUR RIGHTEOUSNESS, or Jehovah our Righteousness. And why? Because he is to be God the mediator, by whose hand we shall obtain [the] righteousness of God. God therefore calls him by the name of Jehovah."[11]

From what has been said, it appears that Jesus Christ the Messiah is Jehovah. For since that title is in Scripture a principal note of distinction by which the true God was pleased to manifest himself and to set forth his own superior excellency in opposition to all pretended deities; and since this name is given to Christ and applied to Christ so frequently; it follows, and the consequence is undeniable, that Christ is that God, that only true God, who is possessed of all those distinguishing powers and perfections which go along with that sublime title.

Jesus Christ is the First and Last.

In the Old Testament	In the New Testament
Isa 44:6. *I am the first and I am the last; besides me there is no god.*	Rev 22:13. *I am the Alpha and the Omega, the first and the last.*[12]

---

[11] Buxtorf, *Lexic.*, 164.
[12] The original reads Rev 1:11 and De Gols was probably thinking of 1:8, but the closest (and actual) text that he quotes is Rev 22:13.

I cited this text of Isaiah before to prove that Christ is Jehovah. Now I reproduce it because it expresses the eternal greatness and infinite majesty of God, and to prove that Christ is that God, because this most glorious title is given to him: a title which expresses the eternity not only of the divine Being, but his supreme power, dignity, and glory, and his government of all things (Isa 44:6-8).

Maimonides[13] tells us, that it is the fourth article of the Jewish Faith to believe, "That God is the First and the Last."[14] But the Gospel has made it the first, the principal, the fundamental article of the Christian Faith, that our Lord Jesus Christ is the first and the last, is the supreme God, with the Father and the Holy Ghost, the only one God.

Jesus Christ is called God absolutely.

In Acts 20:28 we find Christ called God absolutely. *"Care for the church of God, which he obtained with his own blood."* There is also 1Ti 3:16, *"God is manifest in the Flesh."*[15] In both these places the name of God is

---

[13] Moses ben Maimon (1135-1204). Spanish born rabbi who became one of the most influential of all medieval Torah scholars.

[14] Maimon, *Sanh*. C. 10.

[15] The ESV reads, *"He was manifest in the flesh."* There is a textual difficulty here. The pronoun "he" translates a Greek word that has two letters, *o* and *s*. When they are together, this means "who." Many manuscripts have *th* for *o*, making it possible to read *theos* (God). Even though the "who" is almost certainly original, it is still vague. Who is the "who?" It can refer to either God or to Christ (who is also God).

given to Christ in the most strict and proper sense, in the same manner as it is given to the Father.

Jesus Christ is the True God.

1 John 5:20. *"We are in him that is true, even in his Son Jesus Christ."*[16] This is the true God and eternal life. That this was spoken of Jesus Christ is most certain from the scope of the whole Epistle, wherein the Apostle purposed to speak of Christ's divinity; for there were heretics at that time, namely Cerinthus and the Ebonites, who taught that Christ was merely a man. The Apostle, therefore, in opposition to these heretics, asserts this of Jesus Christ, for nobody can doubt it of the Father.

He asserts therefore that Christians are in God, because Jesus Christ is God, and he calls God *"the true"* (*alēthinon*). He then explains that *"even in his Son"* (*en tō huiō autou*) is said here to be the true God and eternal life. This is evident from the pronoun *"this"* (*houtos*). All grammar obliges us to refer that to both predicates.

For these two predicates are of great weight, the first *"this is the true God"* and the next *"and eternal life."* Now it has been acknowledged even by an adversary,

---

[16] The ESV reads, *"So that we may know him who is true, in his Son Jesus Christ."*

that Eternal Life is a name of Jesus Christ,[17] and appropriated to him; and it is as certain that the other predicate pertains to the same Person. For had it been intended of the Father, that he is the true God, and Christ the Eternal Life, the text should have run *houtos*, "this" is the true God, and *ekeinos*, "that" other is Eternal Life; but the words are, "*This is the true God, and Eternal Life.*" There is but one subject to both predicates.

Some copies read the first part of this verse, "*We are in him that is the true God,*" *alēthinon theon*, and this strengthens the Apostle's assertion, for then the sense must be this, "*We know that the Son of God is come, and has given us an understanding that we may know the true God; and we are in him that is the true God, even in his Son Jesus Christ. This is the true God and Eternal Life.*"

This construction most powerfully asserts that there is no way of knowing the true God for certain, except by such a Teacher who is God himself. And Christ has both taught us the true God, and united us to the true God, himself being the true God. This is agreeable to the whole design of St. John, which is both in his Gospel and Epistles to vindicate the divinity of Christ, against the heretics of those times. Therefore, as he began his Gospel, so he ends this Epistle, averting the divine nature of Christ; and in both,

---

[17] *Modest Plea*, 264. Vide Becman. Exercit. X. Amst. 1643. This is most likely the book written by Samuel Clarke.

he frequently inculcates the necessity of believing Christ to be the true God.

Jesus Christ is the Great God and Saviour.

Titus 2:13. "*Waiting for our blessed hope, the appearing of the glory of our great God and Savior Jesus Christ.*" In this text the titles of great God and Savior are given to Christ. That they concern Christ alone is certain because there is no mention of the Father, but only Christ in the following part of the discourse. It is evident further from the article *ta* (*"the"*) which is used only once, whereby one and the same Person only is spoken of. For had two different persons been designed, the article would have been put before "Savior," and because the *epiphaneian* (*"the appearing"*) is always ascribed to the Son alone and never to the Father.[18] Therefore, with submission, the version could and ought to be rendered, "*the glorious appearing of our great God and Saviour Jesus Christ.*" Our old translation, though it does not come up to the force of the Greek, still comes nearer than this one. "*Looking for that blessed hope and appearing of that glory of that mighty God, and of our Saviour Jesus Christ.*" Our adversaries themselves confess that the grammatical construction requires both to be ascribed to Christ.[19]

---

[18] 2Th 2:8; 1Ti 6:14; 2Tim 1:10; 4:1, 8.
[19] Clarke's *Scripture-Doctrine*, 77, 2nd edition.

Jesus Christ is the only Sovereign God and Lord.

Jude 4. "*For certain people have crept in unnoticed ... deny our only Master and Lord, Jesus Christ.*" The one article denotes that Jesus Christ is that only Lord and God. The force of the word *despotēn* ("Master") is not sufficiently explained. The words may thus be rendered, "*that only*" sovereign God and Lord of ours, Jesus Christ. The Complutensian Codex[20] reads it as, "*that only God and our sovereign Lord*" (*ton monon theon kai despotēn ton kurion*), And Mr. Perkins has it, "*the only Ruler who is God, and our Lord Jesus Christ.*"[21]

Jesus Christ is the Mighty God.

Isaiah 9:6. "*His name shall be called Wonderful, Counsellor, the Mighty God.*" Before I explain this text, I must observe that the LXX has everywhere rendered the Hebrew *El* and *Elohim* by "*God*" (*theon*). Aquila has rendered it by *ischuron*, from its proper signification, "*the powerful*" God; though some rather derive it from a word expressing God's omnipresence, according to Jer 23:23. "*Am I a God at hand, declares the LORD, and not a God far away?*" But whatever the etymon (derivation of the word) is, this is the proper name of God,

---

[20] Original note: Beza in loc. Editor's note. Printed 1502-1517, this is the first full polyglot (multiple language side-by-side) Bible ever printed.
[21] [William] Perkins, *Exposit.* in loc.

and St. Jerome says that it is the proper title of the only true God, because he alone possesses almighty power.[22] This is given to the Child Christ Jesus, as well as to the eternal Father.

To the Father	To Christ Jesus
Isa 10:21. *The remnant shall return, even the remnant of Jacob to the mighty God, the El Gibbor.*	Isa 9:6. *Unto us a child is born, a Son is given—and his name shall be the El Gibbor, the mighty God.*

The LXX has taken a strange liberty in translating this, for instead of saying "the mighty God," they have made a comment and turned it into, *"the Angel of the great council"* (*megalēs boulēs aggelos*). St. Jerome thinks the reason was because they thought it was strange to apply the name of God and *"mighty"* to a child.[23] Some are of the opinion that the latter Jews had corrupted some copies of the LXX, and that after this several of the most ancient Christian writers, who highly valued the Septuagint version, quoted this text, not as that has it, but as it is in the Hebrew text.[24] And as this name of *El* is given to Christ in the singular, so it is also in the plural number.

---

[22] Jerome, in *Esa.*, 85. Ed. Bened.
[23] Jerome, in Esa., 86.
[24] Dr. Waterland, *Sermon* 6, 219. This is Daniel Waterland (1683-1740), an English theologian who became Master of Magdalene College, Cambridge in 1714, Chancellor of the Diocese of York in 1722, and Archdeacon of Middlesex in 1730.

Jesus Christ is Jehovah Elohim, the Lord God,
and El Elohim, the God of gods.

This word [Elohim] is used in the plural, both to denote the Trinity of Persons in the unity of the divine Essence, as also to signify the exceeding greatness of God's power; and though it is given sometimes analogically to angels and princes,[25] it is notwithstanding the proper name of God.

This name is construed with a verb of the singular number, and has the name of Jehovah added to it, to denote the Trinity of Persons in the unity of the Divinity.[26]

This name is given to Christ (Ps 48:8, 9, 10). "*As we have heard, so we have seen in the city of the Lord of hosts, in the city of our God, which God will establish forever. Selah. We have thought on your steadfast love, O God, in the midst of your temple. As your Name, O God, so your praise…*" Here the name of Elohim is given to Christ four times, and twice in the last verse. "*This is God, our God forever and ever. He will guide us forever* (KJV: *unto death*)." And so again in Hosea 1:7, "*I will have mercy on the house of Judah, and I will save them by the LORD their God,*" by "*Jehovah their Elohim.*" The Jews themselves acknowledge this text is about the Messiah, and accordingly the Chaldee paraphrase [that is, the Targum] reads it, "*by his Word which is their God.*"

---

[25] Psalm 96:5; The original reads 97:5 (a typo). It also has Gen 6:13 and Ex 4:5, both of which are inexplicable.
[26] He cites here Johannes Hoornbeck (1617-1666), *Confut. Socin.* 1.2.c.5., p. 420.

In the New Testament we find the same title of *"Lord God"* given to Christ (Luke 1:16, 17). We find the angel speaking of John the Baptist, *"And he will turn many of the children of Israel to the Lord their God, and he will go before him,"* namely before Christ, who is that Lord God. In the strictest construction, the words *"Lord their God"* are so immediately connected to *"him,"* that they cannot possibly be understood of any person but Christ. If this is compared with Luke 3:4 and Malachi 3:1, it is impossible that any person can be understood but Christ, who is the Lord.

As Christ is called *Jehovah Elohim, "the Lord God,"* so he is also called *El Elohim, "the God of Gods."* Ps 50:1, as our old translation has it, is a Psalm that has always been looked upon as relating to Christ and his coming to judgment, and as such it must necessarily pertain to Christ. *"For the Father judges no one but has given all judgment to the Son"* (John 5:22). And so the Psalmist speaks to Christ, *"Arise, O God, and judge the earth"* (Ps 82:8). Upon this text the Jews have this comment, "When the judgment goes forth in mercy and favor, the Judge is called Jehovah; but when he punishes, he is called Elohim."[27]

Jesus Christ is over all God blessed forever.

Rom 9:5. *"To them belong the patriarchs, and from their race, according to the flesh, is the Christ, who is God*

---

[27] Buxtorf, *Lexicon*, 30.

over all, blessed forever. Amen." That St. Paul speaks this of Christ is so plain from the whole context that no expression whatsoever could be plainer; for the Father is not so much as named in the foregoing part of the chapter. And "*who is*" (*ho ōn*) naturally refers to the person spoken of immediately before it, and that is Christ. The antithesis between what he is according to the flesh and according to the Spirit requires it.

It is pretended as an objection to the force of this text that some manuscripts read, "*who is over all blessed forever,*" without the word God; and that Erasmus has observed that some of the Fathers do not have the word "*God*" in this text.[28]

But Dr. Mill[29] says that the manuscripts have it, as also the Syriac version; and Erasmus,[30] his pretense from the Fathers is vain, for he names but two, only Cyprian and Hilary, and are they of weight against the whole Catholic[31] church? And as Beza[32] has observed, though

---

[28] Metzger's discussion of this verse is lengthy, but only because the punctuation is difficult. There is no hint that the word "God" does not belong in the passage according to modern scholars.

[29] John Mill, *in loc.*

[30] Erasmus *in loc.*

[31] Original note: "That the Word of God was in the Greek copies in the time of Noetus, is evident from his quoting the text with it at his second appearance." Epiph. *Haer.* 57. P. 114. Edit. Billii Col. Agrip. 1617. Editor's note. "Catholic" refers not to Rome but to "universal" here. Noetus was a presbyter in Asia Minor around 230 A.D. and was a proponent of the heresy called modalistic Monarchianism or Patripassianism. Epiphanius of Salamis (310-403 A.D) was a bishop of Salamis, Cyprus and defended the orthodox faith against heresies. His work *Panarion* (also known as Adversus Haereses or "Against Heresies") is what De Gols is citing here.

[32] Beza, in loc.

the word God is not in the text, the sense would be the same, and the divinity of Christ sufficiently expressed by "*being over all,*" and by "*blessed forever.*" I will not turn to the significance of these phrases.

Our author pretends from the Socinians that this is a doxology, and that it is a form used by the Jews, God be blessed forever; and therefore, the evidence of this text vanishes by an ellipsis.[33]

That the Jews used such a form is true, but that this is the case here, all the figures of speech in the world can never make out, and nothing but open violence to grammar can pretend to be done to the text. When all is done, all they do is make the sense broken and confused, for neither the grammar nor the antithesis will allow such an ellipsis. The antithesis absolutely requires that both the divine and human natures should be expressed. This is what we find in Romans 1:3 where he says that, "*Christ was made of the Seed of*" David. In Romans 9:5 he says, "*of the Fathers,*" but in both it reads "*according to the flesh*" (*kata sarka*), creating the parallel. Again, in 1:3 it says that he was "*declared with power to the Son of God according to the Spirit of Holiness*" (*kata pneuma agiōsunēs*), and in 9:5 that he is "*over all God blessed forever.*" So that this is no doxology, but a plain description of the divine nature of Jesus Christ,

---

[33] William Staunton, *The Sincere Thoughts of a Private Christian*, 63. An ellipsis is the omission from speech or writing of a word or words that are superfluous or able to be understood from contextual clues.

such that as certain as he is of the Father, so surely is Jesus Christ *"over all God blessed forever."*

Having defended the text, I will now show you the significance of the expression *"over all God blessed forever,"* which is the most lofty expression that can be made; for Christ is not only here called God, but God with the most exalted epithet, "over all," even as it is given to God the Father.

To the Father	To the Son
Eph 4:6. *One God and Father of all, who is above all.*	Rom 9:5. *Christ, who is over all God blessed forever.*

Besides this, he is called "blessed forever," (*eulogētos eis tous aiōnas*); which is also exactly the same as is given to God the Father.

To the Father	To the Son
Rom 1:25. *The Creator who is blessed forever, Amen.*	Rom 9:5. *Christ, who is God blessed forever, Amen.*

Here we must observe that this phrase *"blessed forever"* was always used by the Jews as a name of God. Through it they expressed the One God of Israel.[34] Therefore, there were no other words to express the divinity of Christ. This alone should be enough to

---

[34] Bishop Pearson, *On The Creed*, Art. 2, p. 133. Bishop Bull, *Defense of the Nicene Creed.* S.2.C.3.§10. This is John Pearson (1613-1686), Bishop of Chester and George Bull (1634-1710), Bishop of St. David's.

prove the point; for according to the Jewish phrase, which the Jews certainly understood, he is God, that is "*blessed forever*," and he that is "*blessed forever*" is most certainly God.

In the Old Testament	In the New Testament
Ps 24:8. *Who is this King of glory? The LORD, strong and mighty, the LORD mighty in battle! ... Who is this King of glory? The LORD of hosts, he is the King of glory.*	1Co 2:8. *None of the rulers of this age understood this, for if they had, they would not have crucified the Lord of God of glory.*

Jesus Christ is King of Kings, and Lord of Lords.

With these titles St. Paul makes the distinguishing characters of the one true God; and these are given and ascribed to the Son, with the same pomp and magnificence, as they are to the Father.

To the Father	To the Son
1Ti 6:15. *He who is the blessed and only Sovereign, the King of kings and Lord of lords.*	Rev 17:14. *The Lamb will conquer them, for he is Lord of lords and King of kings."*
	Rev 19:16. *On his robe and on his thigh he has a name written, "King of kings and Lord of lords."*

Jesus Christ is Life.

This title, which is not the least of God's glorious titles, is equally ascribed to Jesus Christ as to the Father.

To the Father	To the Son
John 5:26. *The Father has life in himself.*	Rev 5:26. *As the Father has life in himself, so he has granted the Son also to have life in himself.*
Dt 32:40. *I live forever.*[35]	
Jer 10:10. *The LORD is the true God; he is the living God.*	Job 19:25. *I know that my Redeemer lives.*
	John 1:4. In him was life.
	John 11:25. *I am ... the life.*
	Acts 3:15. *The Author of life.*

Jesus Christ is the Fullness of the Godhead.

Col 2:9. "*For in him the whole fullness of deity dwells bodily.*" These words of St. Paul are very extraordinary; for the Apostle, foreseeing that heretics would arise that should speak of a secondary God, a God made of a creature, he purposely expressed himself in in this way concerning Christ's divinity, so that we would understand him to be the real and true God, the very supreme God, and not a nominal or contrived god. The Apostle therefore did not say that Christ was

---

[35] Editor's note. I would tend to think that this one is about the Son, not the Father, for the verse has the Person lifting up his hand to heaven and swearing that he will carry out vengeance upon his enemies. This is the duty of the Captain of the Host, the Angel of the LORD.

God, because that word might be liable to exception, having been given to men, princes, and prophets;[36] but to put that matter above all exception, he says that in Jesus all the fullness of the Godhead dwelt bodily; and although he appeared as a man, he was God also; for he expresses two natures in the same Person, the divine inhabiting and the human inhabited.

St. Paul did not say *plērōma theotētos*, which might have been understood for the "fullness" of gifts and graces, wisdom, power, mercy, and the like, a fullness of gifts greater than any created being enjoyed. He expressly says, *tēs theotētos*, of the very Godhead, of the Divinity itself. This is a distinguishing expression. The other signifies the qualities. This the very essence of Divinity, but more, he speaks of the fullness of the Godhead, to let us know that Christ is in all respects the very God, the eternal and supreme God. He then adds *pan to plērōma*, "all the fullness" of the Godhead, to assure us that as the Father is, so also is the Son; and that the Godhead of the Father and of the Son is all one, the glory equal, the majesty co-eternal.

Secondly, that Christ is the very God that is to be worshiped, appears from:

---

[36] A good case can be made that the term "god" is never used of human beings anywhere in the Bible. It is, however, used of various supernatural beings (with a little "g"). See Cyrus Gordon, "אלהים (Elohim) in Its Reputed Meaning of *Rulers, Judges*," *Journal of Biblical Literature* 54 (1935): 139–144.

The Divine Attributes.

By the word "attributes" I mean such perfections and excellencies of the divine Nature, where God is distinguished from the creatures, and where God makes himself known to his creatures. Now these are all ascribed to Christ.

First, Eternity is ascribed to Jesus Christ.[37]

Rev 1:8. *"'I am the Alpha and the Omega,' says the Lord God, 'who is and who was and who is to come, the Almighty.'"* This is the very description which the prophet gives to the one God of Israel (Isa 43:10).[38] But having spoken to this before, I pass to other texts.

Micah 5:2. *"But you, O Bethlehem Ephrathah, who are too little to be among the clans of Judah, from you shall come forth for me one who is to be ruler in Israel, whose coming forth is from of old, from ancient days."* In these words, we plainly find two "comings-forth," the one promised to be in Bethlehem, the other from eternity. This is not only a plain proof that Christ was pre-existing before his birth of the virgin but is as full a proof as words can express of his eternity also.

---

[37] In this and the following sections on the attributes of God, De Gols cites Johannis Marckii's Latin *Compendium theologiæ Christianæ*, 1690 ed.

[38] The original has Isa 43:20. This is a typo. It is probably 43:10.

Prov 8:22-23. *"But you, O Bethlehem Ephrathah, who are too little to be among the clans of Judah, from you shall come forth for me one who is to be ruler in Israel, whose coming forth is from of old, from ancient days."* I will speak more of this text later.

Jesus Christ is Omnipresent.

This is the divine perfection where God cannot be contained by any kind of created thing; he cannot be created; he is present with all creatures; and he infinitely exceeds the limits of the creatures. And so, the third article of the Jewish Faith, expresses God's ubiquity [omnipresence]. "I perfectly believe, that the Creator is not a body. Neither can he be known or understood by any bodily comprehensions. There is nothing else like him."[39]

This is ascribed to God the Father, and also in the same manner to God the Son.

To the Father	To the Son
Jer 23:23-24. *"Am I a God at hand, declares the LORD, and not a God far away? Can a man hide himself in secret places so that I cannot see him?"* declares the LORD. *"Do I not fill*	Matt 18:20. *Where two or three are gathered in my name, there am I among them.* Matt 28:20. *Behold, I am with you always, to the end of the age.*

---

[39] Maimonid. *In Sanhedr*. C. 10.

heaven and earth? declares the LORD."

Acts 17:28. *In him we live and move and have our being.*

Col 1:17. *In him all things hold together.*

Heb 1:3. *He upholds the universe.*

Jesus Christ is Immutable.

Immutability is that most perfect constancy of God whereby he is perfectly free from all change actual or possible. This is God's prerogative, and is ascribed to the Son, in the same pomp and magnificence, as it is to the Father.

To the Father

Ps 102:25-27. *Of old you laid the foundation of the earth, and the heavens are the work of your hands. They will perish, but you will remain; they will all wear out like a garment. You will change them like a robe, and they will pass away, but you are the same, and your years have no end.*

James 1:17. *The Father of lights, with whom there is no variation or shadow due to change.*

To the Son

Heb 1:10-12. *You, Lord, laid the foundation of the earth in the beginning, and the heavens are the work of your hands; they will perish, but you remain; they will all wear out like a garment, like a robe you will roll them up, like a garment they will be changed. But you are the same, and your years will have no end.*

Mal 3:6. *I am the LORD, I do not change.*

Before I proceed, let me make a remark on those admirable words of David (Ps 102) applied by St. Paul to Christ. No words can be devised that more emphatically describe the eternity and immutability of the one only true and eternal God. since they are here ascribed, and that by an Apostle, without any reserve, without the least restriction to Jesus Christ, we are obliged to believe that this Jesus Christ is the eternal and immutable God. When David first expressed these words, he spoke of Jehovah, the God of Israel. When the Apostle applies them, it is to Christ. The great actions mentioned there are the actions of Christ He expands the heavens and lays the foundations of the earth. Those great attributes of the divine Nature there related, namely immutability and eternity, are the perfections of Jesus Christ. Christ therefore is Jehovah, the God of Israel, the one and only God, as well as the Father.

It is very observable that this text is co-penned by the sacred writer and that therefore all reasons for criticism of prepositions or articles are prevented. Whatever doubt there may be by them, or because of them in other texts, there can be none in this—Christ is the eternal God, Christ is God immutable.

Jesus Christ is the Independent God

Independency is that perfection of God where he is sufficient in himself and is the only cause of all things. It is a divine perfection that declares the all-sufficiency and happiness of the divine Nature. This is ascribed to the Son equally as to the Father.

To the Father	To the Son
Gen 17:1. *"I am the Almighty God;"* or, as the old translation has it, according to the Hebrews, *"I am the all-sufficient."*	John 5:26. *As the Father has life in himself, so he has granted the Son also to have life in himself.*

This text of St. John is very well worthy of our consideration, as it does most admirably assert Christ's divinity, and explain his independency. This text clearly intimates that although he had his divine life and nature from the Father, as the fountain of the Deity, yet he received it not by participation, but by communication. He did not only participate of it, but it was wholly communicated to him. Hence, the Christian Fathers have called Christ "self-perfection," self-power," "self-God," "self-light," "self-understanding," and the like.[40]

All of these expressions, Epiphanius seems to explain most clearly, plainly showing that those expressions signify not that Christ has them of himself, but in himself, and that though he is God of God, yet he is God in himself.[41] This is sufficient to title him "Self-

---

[40] Gregory of Nyssa, *Catech. Major.* Basil, 1.2. *Contra Eunomium*, 740. Tom. I. Ed. Par. 1638.
[41] Epiph. *Haer.* 77. P. 243. Edit. Colon. 1617.

God," one who is God in himself, and so is God himself; not another God, but another Person from the Father, having the same Essence communicated to him.

Jesus Christ is the Omniscient God.

Omniscience is that perfection of God where he most perfectly knows all things in himself, by one eternal act. This is most certainly a divine perfection, and the divine privilege; and is in the Scriptures ascribed to the Son equally as to the Father.

To the Father	To the Son
1Kg 8:39. *For you, you only, know the hearts of all the children of mankind.*	John 16:30. *Now we know that you know all things.*
Acts 15:8. *God, who knows the heart.*	John 21:17. *Lord, you know everything.*
Jer 17:10. *I the LORD search the heart and test the mind.*	Rev 2:23. *I am he who searches mind and heart.*
	Acts 1:24. *You, Lord, who know the hearts of all.*
	Col 2:3. *In whom are hidden all the treasures of wisdom and knowledge.*

Jesus Christ is the Almighty God.

Omnipotence is a divine attribute according to all men. It is the perfection of the Son as well as of the Father. The Scriptures assure us of this, as they ascribe it to the Father and to the Son with the same strength of expression.

Before I show you that it is applied to the Son, I must observe, that the word "Almighty," (*pantokratōr*), translates the Hebrew *Shadday*, the all-sufficient (Gen 17:1). It also translates another phrase used in Scripture to express almighty power, and that is the Lord of Hosts, *Jehovah Sabaoth*. St. Ambrose and Jerome[42] have observed that the LXX has rendered Jehovah Sabaoth indifferently by the Lord of Hosts and Almighty. And St. John in Revelation 4:8 alludes to the thrice holy of Isaiah (6:3). Instead of (*kurios sabaōth*), as the Septuagint has it,[43] which is "*Lord of Hosts,*" it has "*Lord God Almighty*" (*kurios o theos o pantokratōr*).

That this attribute is the property of the Father needs no proof; but that it is applied only to the Father is not true, for it is applied to the Son both in the Old and New Testaments.

To the Father	To the Son
Isa 6:5. *Woe is me … for my eyes have seen the*	John 12:41. *Isaiah said these things because he saw (Christ) his glory and spoke of him.* John 19:34, 37. *One of the soldiers pierced his side with a spear …*

---

[42] Ambrose, *de fide*, l.4. c. 1. P. 314. Edit. Par. Anno 1569; Jerome, tom. 3. P. 519.

[43] De Gols says the LXX reads, *kurios dunameōn*. But there are not variants that have this reading.

King, the LORD of hosts![44] *Zech 12:5, 10. The inhabitants of Jerusalem have strength through the LORD of hosts, their God ... I will pour out on the house of David and the inhabitants of Jerusalem a spirit of grace and pleas for mercy, so that, when they look on me, on him whom they have pierced.*[45]

Against another Scripture says, "They will look on him whom they have pierced." Rev 1:7-8. Behold, he is coming with the clouds, and every eye will see him, even those who pierced him, and all tribes of the earth will wail on account of him. Even so. Amen. "I am the Alpha and the Omega," says the Lord God, "who is and who was and who is to come, the Almighty."

Thirdly, that Christ is the very God and is therefore to be worshiped appears from:

The Divine Operations.

All the works of God are ascribed to Christ in the same manner as they are to the Father. John 5:19, *"Truly, truly, I say to you, the Son can do nothing of his own accord, but only what he sees the Father doing. For whatever the Father does, that the Son does likewise."*

---

[44] This is not a good proof-text for the Father, as Jesus says Isaiah saw him (John 12:41). Curiously, this is the passage that De Gols cites right beside it for the Son.

[45] This verse is also cited in the NT as referring to Christ rather than the Father, and therefore would seem not to be referring to the Father (John 19:37). Again, De Gols cites the NT quotation for Christ. De Gols seems to imply that the NT is changing the meaning from the Father to the Son.

The adversaries of the divinity of Christ make use of this very text against Christ as an argument against his almighty power. But then, I must observe to you that they divide the text and take only the first part. Be well assured, they do not take it as it is. It is most positively against them. The full meaning of the text is that God the Son is intimately united with the Father, never separate from him, and therefore never acts except in concert with him. Their operation is undivided, and their work is one. Then it appears that this text is so far from denoting any imperfection in the power of the Son, that, on the contrary, it sets forth the greatness and unmeasurable perfection of his power as being inseparably linked with, and indeed one and the same in extent and degree, with the power of the Father.

Jesus Christ is the Creator of the World.

That the creating of the world is an act of God, of Almighty power is a truth known to all mankind and acknowledged by the very light of nature. This is ascribed to Jesus Christ in the Scriptures exactly as it is to the eternal Father.

To the Father	To the Son
Gen 1:1. *In the beginning God created the heaven and the earth.*	John 1:3, 10. *All things were made through him (Christ the Word) and without him was not*

Ex 20:11. *In six days the LORD made heaven and earth, the sea, and all that is in them.*

2Kg 19:15. *You are the God, you alone, of all the kingdoms of the earth; you have made heaven and earth.*

Heb 3:4. *The builder of all things is God.*

anything made that was made … He was in the world, and the world was made through him.

Col 1:15-17. *He is the image of the invisible God, the firstborn of all creation. For by him all things were created, in heaven and on earth, visible and invisible, whether thrones or dominions or rulers or authorities—all things were created through him and for him. And he is before all things, and in him all things hold together.*

Before I proceed, I must observe that several of the ancients, namely Origen, Basil, and Ambrose, have rendered the word *reshith* in Gen 1:1 as *"The Beginning," "by the Son."*[46] And, the Chaldee Paraphrase

---

[46] Jerome says, "Most people think that in the Hebrew is contained in the Son, God made heaven and earth" (Jerome, *Questions in Hebrew,* in Genesis ii. 507. Quoted in Saint Jerome's, *Hebrew Questions on Genesis,* trans. C. T. R. Hayward [Oxford: Oxford University Press, 1995], 30).

The Fathers get it from the meaning of *reshith* as either "beginning" or "first." What if the Hebrew was talking about first as preeminence? The word carries this meaning in places in the OT. *"Amalek was the first (reshith) among the nations"* (Num 24:20). *"[Leviathan] is the first of the works of God"* (Job 40:19). Sometimes the first-born was the *reshith* as in *"Reuben, you are my first-born (bekor); My might and the beginning (reshith) of my strength"* (Gen 49:3). Paul seems to be taking very Jewish ideas like this and applying them to Jesus at creation when he says, *"He is the image of the invisible God, the firstborn of all creation. For by him all things were created, in heaven and on earth, visible and invisible, whether thrones of dominions or rulers or authorities—all things were created through him and for him. And he is before all things, and in him all things hold together"* (Col 1:15-17). So the translation idea of Genesis 1:1 is that In the First, that is in the Firstborn Son, God began creating.

(i.e. the Targum) for *in principio*, in the Beginning, has in *Sapentia*, on or by his Wisdom. This Wisdom is the Logos, the Son of God, and this agrees excellently well with Solomon in Prov 8:22. "*The LORD possessed me (reshith darko)*, "*the beginning of his way*" (*principium via suae*), that is, of his works, as Vatablus[47] expounds it. The text makes it good, for the same verse has, "*I was before his works of old*;" where the Word *qedem* adverbially signifies "before," as we have rendered it, but substantively signifies an orientation, i.e. the "*sunrise of his words of old.*" There is no necessity to make *reshith* an adverb either, as they are both substantives. Therefore *reshith* is the essential Wisdom of God, not a property but a substance; for true Wisdom is substance, according to Plotinus, "The true wisdom is substance and the true substance is wisdom." This substantial Wisdom is the Logos, Jesus Christ, the Son of God, called by St. Paul, "*The firstborn of every creature.*" This is the Wisdom of God, or the idea according to which he framed all things, and therefore must be before all things. Answerable to this are the two attributes Philo gives to the same subject, calling him "the firstborn Word of God" (*prologonon theos logon*) and "*the Beginning*" (*archēn*).[48]

---

[47] François Vatable (d. 1547) was a French humanist scholar, a Hellenist, and a Hebraist.
[48] De Gols cites Henry More (1614-1687) here and his work on the Cabala.

I must observe further that our translation, which has rendered by *"the firstborn of every creature"* (*prōtotokos pasēs ktiseōs*), does not come up to the force of the Greek; for the original signifies *"firstborn before all the creation"* (Col 1:15). And St. Paul himself shows it must be so understood, because in vs. 17 he says, *"He is before all things,"* which positively exempts him from being one of the creatures, because *"all things were made by him."* Therefore, our version ought to be corrected, with submission to grammar and consistency in this place, as it is does not agree with the text, and as it may give a foothold to our adversaries to believe Christ to be a created being, though the first of the creation. St. Paul intended to signify the exact opposite, that Christ is no creature. this is so far from the firstborn of every creature that he existed before all things, and that all the creatures in heaven and earth were made and created by him.

- Eph 3:9. *"God, who created all things by Jesus Christ."*[49]
- Heb 1:2. *"Through whom also he created the world."*
- 1Co 8:6. *"To us there is one God, the Father, from whom are all things and for whom we exist, and one*

---

[49] Some manuscripts do not have "by Christ Jesus." The ESV follows that tradition.

Lord, Jesus Christ, through whom are all things and through whom we exist."

In this last text, St. Paul opposes both Father and Son to the many gods and many lords. There is but one Lord to us, namely Jesus Christ. Does this mean that the Father is excluded among the many Lords, since he is also the Lord *"by whom are all things"* (Rom 11:34, 36)? God forbid, but Father and Son are one Lord. So again, to us there is but one God, namely the Father.

Is the Son then excluded among the many gods, since it is the Son who *"is over all, God blessed forever"* (Rom 9:5)? God forbid, but Father and Son are one God. For St. Paul in this place not only tells us that the Father and Son are one God and one Lord, but also intimates the reason why. For this reason they are one—because all things flow from both. There is nothing of the Father but by the Son; nor any thing by the Son but what is also of the Father, so that the original of all creatures is referred to both, as to one individual fountain and cause of their existence.

I must further observe, that the expressions "in him" (*en autō*), "by him" (*di autou*), and "for him" (*eis auton*) are used both in respect to the Father as to the Son. So also *eis auton ta panta* and *di autou ta panta* are equally applied to the Father and to the Son, *"all things are for him, and all things are by him."* These expressions are equally applied to Father and Son and did not drop by chance from the pen of inspired writers, but they have a certain and full meaning to signify that these two Persons are the same God and Creator. As a consequence, this effectually takes off any pretense the Arians [those who taught that Christ is only a human] can have merely from the force of the prepositions, as if they were intended for a note of inferiority, when they are nothing more than a note of distinction. The operation of one is of equal extent with the operation of the other. Indeed, all is but one work of both.

Before I leave this matter, I shall only mention[50] that the work of creation is everywhere represented as the certain mark or characteristic of the true God. It is the favorite topic which God is pleased to insist most upon, whenever he would either distinguish his own peculiar majesty and power above and beyond all the gods of the nations; or when he would excite in his people the highest idea possible, suitable to his transcendent excellency, and peerless perfections.

For instance, Isaiah 40:26. *"Lift up your eyes on high and see: who created these? He who brings out their host by number."* And Job 12:7-9. *"But ask the beasts, and they will teach you; the birds of the heavens, and they will tell you; or the bushes of the earth, and they will teach you; and the fish of the sea will declare to you. Who among all these does not know that the hand of the LORD has done this?"*

---

[50] Dr. Waterland, *On the Divinity of Christ*, Sermon 3, p. 93.

Creation is the distinguishing character of the one true God. Whenever the Scripture intended to raise in men's minds such esteem and veneration as they ought to have for the supreme God, nothing higher nor greater could be said than this, that he is the Creator, that he created the universe, that he had laid the foundations of the earth, and that the heavens are the works of his hands. Therefore Socinus, to evade the force of that argument and of the consequence St. Paul draws from it for divine worship (Rom 1:25), fell into this mad notion that God is not to be known from the creation.[51] After him, others followed.

But if some are so blind that they cannot see, and others so prejudiced that they will not see, they are but few; and these perhaps express their wishes rather than their thoughts, and are no argument against universal consent; unless we must conclude that nature is not regular in its course, because it produces some monsters and prodigies. No! These few are rather to be deemed delirious than that all the world should be fools.

Jesus Christ is the Preserver of the World.

Although preservation is always included in creation, as it is in a sense a continual creation, the Scriptures have often singled it out by name and laid a very

---

[51] Socinus, *prolect.* Cs2. *"Negamus Deum aliquo modo ex operibus agnosci posse."*

great stress upon it. Therefore, I thought it best to mention it by it itself.

This is a divine act which none but infinite power can perform; for there is no less power and wisdom and goodness in the preservation of the creatures than in their first creation, and God is as greatly to be praised for our well-being as for our initial being. The Scholastics have happily called this *manutenentia*, that is a continual holding his hand to his work; for should God withdraw his aid, how soon would all things perish?

This act of divine power and mercy is ascribed to God the Father. So it is also, with great force and emphasis, ascribed to God the Son in the holy Scriptures.

To the Father	To the Son
Neh 9:6. *You are the LORD, you alone. You have made heaven, the heaven of heavens, with all their host, the earth and all that is on it, the seas and all that is in them; and you preserve all of them.* Ps 36:6. *Man and beast you preserve, O LORD.* Ps 145:15. *The eyes of all look to you, and you give them their food in due season.*	John 5:17. *My Father is working until now, and I am working.* Col 1:17. *In him all things hold together.*

Jesus Christ is the Worker of Miracles.

The working of miracles has been esteemed by all men to be the peculiar prerogative of God, because no

Ch. 5 – That Divine Worship is Due Christ   **51**

one but he has the springs of nature in his hands; and only he can bend them to such ends, as his will and wisdom shall direct them. Miracles are such acts which are above and contrary to the course of nature. The holy Scriptures ascribe them to God and God alone. Yet, they also ascribe them to Jesus Christ, the Son of God, as a demonstration of his almighty power, and his divine nature, that he with the Father is that One only God.

To the Father	To the Son
Ps 72:18. *Blessed be the LORD, the God of Israel, who alone does wondrous things.*	Luke 6:19. *For power came out of him and healed them all.*
Ps 86:10. *For you are great and do wondrous things; you alone are God.*	Matt 11:5. *The blind receive their sight and the lame walk, lepers are cleansed and the deaf hear, and the dead are raised up, and the poor have good news preached to them.*
Ps 136:4. *O give thanks ... to him who alone does great wonders.*	
1Co 12:6. *And there are varieties of activities, but it is the same God who empowers them all in everyone.*	

And Christ not only brought about miracles himself, but as a further demonstration of his divinity, he empowered his Apostles to do the same.

- Luke 10:19. *"Behold, I give unto you authority to tread on serpents and scorpions, and over all the power of the enemy."*

- Acts 4:10. *"Let it be known to all of you and to all the people of Israel that by the name of Jesus Christ of Nazareth, whom you crucified, whom God raised from the dead-- by him this man is standing before you well."*

Jesus Christ is the God of all Mercy & Grace, the Redeemer.

The word grace not only signifies pity and compassion, but aid and assistance which we receive from God. Through it, we are enabled to do those things that please God. It also signifies the whole work of redemption and all the blessings and favors which flow from it, which God was pleased to effect by Jesus Christ.

Redemption is the highest act of God's wisdom, power, and mercy. It is an act far exceeding the work of creation. In the creation there was nothing to withstand almighty power; God spoke, and it was done: *"He commanded, and they were created"* (Ps 32:9; cf. Ps 148:5). But in the redemption, God's justice was to be satisfied. His law, which was violated by man's transgression, was to be fulfilled. Atonement was to be made for transgressors, before mankind could be received into favor and God become gracious to them. For God is a law to himself, his attributes are a rule and measure to his works. God set forth Christ Jesus therefore, *"For a demonstration of his righteousness against sin"* and *"God made him to be sin for us who knew no sin, that we might be made the righteousness of God in him"* (Rom 3:25; 2Co 5:21).

As this is the highest demonstration of God's love, that he *"gave his Son for our redemption"* (John 3:16), so the whole act of redemption by Christ is the demonstration of the sublimest wisdom and the greatest power. Thus, Christ is called both the Wisdom and Power of God (1Co 1:24).

And as it was only God's power that could redeem mankind, so the Scriptures, God's revelation of that redemption, ascribe it to God only, yet both to the Father and to the Son, including the Holy Ghost, who are that one God who has redeemed us.

To the Father

Isa 63:16. *For you are our Father, our Redeemer.*

Eph 2:4-5. *But God, being rich in mercy, because of the great love with which he loved us, even when we were dead in our trespasses, made us alive together with Christ.*

Hos 1:7. *But I will have mercy on the house of Judah, and I will save them by the LORD their God.*

Luke 1:68. *Blessed be the Lord God of Israel, for he has visited and redeemed his people.*

To the Son

Isa 25:9. *It will be said on that day, "Behold, this is our God; we have waited for him, that he might save us. This is the LORD; we have waited for him; let us be glad and rejoice in his salvation."*

Acts 20:28. *Care for the church of God, which he obtained with his own blood.*

1Co 1:30. *Because of him you are in Christ Jesus, who became to us wisdom from God, righteousness and sanctification and redemption.*

John 1:16. *For from his fullness we have all received, grace upon grace.*

Jesus Christ is the God that Forgives Sins.

"*Sin is lawlessness*" (1Jn 3:4). The law is God's image, his will. Therefore, all sin is against God, and it is God's right and privilege alone to forgive sins. So, the holy Scriptures ascribe it only to God, as an act of God and of God alone. Yet, this they ascribe both to Father and Son and also to the Holy Ghost, who are that one and only God.

To the Father	To the Son
Ex 34:6-7. *The LORD, the LORD, a God merciful and gracious, slow to anger, and abounding in steadfast love and faithfulness, keeping steadfast love for thousands, forgiving iniquity and transgression and sin.* Isa 43:25. *I, I am he who blots out your transgressions for my own sake, and I will not remember your sins.* Jer 31:34. *I will forgive their iniquity, and I will remember their sin no more.* Luke 5:21. *Who can forgive sins but God alone?*	Matt 9:2, 6. *Take heart, my son; your sins are forgiven. ... But that you may know that the Son of Man has authority on earth to forgive sins—he then said to the paralytic—"Rise, pick up your bed and go home."* Matt 26:28. *This is my blood of the covenant, which is poured out for many for the forgiveness of sins.* Col 1:14. *In whom we have redemption, the forgiveness of sins.*

Jesus Christ is God who Regenerates and Sanctifies.

Regeneration and sanctification are as much out of man's power as his creation. Men, spiritually dead in sin, can no more raise themselves to a new life than a man naturally dead can raise himself to natural life. Regeneration is the gift of God and of God alone; and the holy Scripture ascribes it to God alone, as his own act and deed and his alone. Yet, it is ascribed to God the Father and in the same manner to God the Son, who, with the Holy Ghost, is that one God who is the Lord and Giver of Life.

To the Father	**To the Son**
1Th 5:23. *Now may the God of peace himself sanctify you completely.*	John 17:19. *For their sake I consecrate myself, that they also may be sanctified in truth.*
	1Co 6:2. *You were sanctified, you were justified in the Name of the Lord Jesus Christ and by the Spirit of our God.*
	Heb 2:11. *He who sanctifies and those who are sanctified all have one source. That is why he is not ashamed to call them brothers.*

Jesus Christ is God the Sanctifier.

Therefore St. Paul calls Christ the *"Lord from heaven,"* and the *"quickening Spirit,"* when he compares him to the first Adam (1Co 15:22). *"For as in Adam all die, so also in Christ shall all be made alive."* How so? Because Christ is the *"Lord from heaven"* (vs. 47), and in vs. 45 he is *"the quickening Spirit;"* where the expressions

"The Lord from heaven" (*ho kurios*[52] *ex ouranou*) and "the quickening Spirit" (*pneuma zōopoioun*) signify his divine Nature and can signify nothing else.

For that "*Lord from heaven*" signifies God is beyond dispute and appears evidently from John 3:31, "*He who comes from above is above all … He who comes from heaven is above all.*" The Jews used to call God, "*The Adam above who is blessed,*" and the Cabalists say that this "*Adam above*" was married to the "*congregation of Israel,*" where the marriage between Adam and Eve was a representation. This is what St. Paul applies "*to Christ and his church*" (Eph 5:32).[53]

The other phrase also signifies the divinity of Christ; for in this verse Adam, who was only a man, is fully distinguished from the last Adam, who was more than a man, who was also God. "*The first man Adam was made a living soul, the last Adam was made a life-giving Spirit*" (1Co 15:45). In both the Scriptures and the ancient Jews, by "Spirit" refers to the divine Nature of the Messiah; for this is how they interpret Gen 1:2: "The Spirit of the Lord moved upon the face of the waters … This is the Spirit of King Messiah."[54]

---

[52] *Ho kurios* ("the Lord") is only found in some manuscripts. Thus, if you took out an ESV, you would not read "the Lord from heaven," but the "man from heaven." Though a disputed reading, the theology is certainly not disputed.

[53] Bishop Bull, *Jud. Eccl. Cath.* C.5.§.5.

[54] John Lightfoot, *A Commentary on the New Testament from the Talmud and Hebraica, Matthew–1 Corinthians, Acts–1 Corinthians*, vol. 4 (Bellingham, WA: Logos Bible Software, 2010), 274.

Jesus Christ is God, the Judge of the World.

That God is judge of the whole world is a truth we have received from God, not merely by revelation, but God has imprinted it in the law of nature and wrote it in the hearts of all mankind.[55] That God alone is judge is as certain, and the Scriptures have ascribed the judgment to God, both to the Father and to the Son as God, as that one God.

Because the judgment is to be executed in a visible manner, the Scripture tells us that God has appointed Jesus Christ the Son of God, and the Son of Man, God and man, to hold that judgment visibly. *"For the Father judges no man but has committed all judgment to the Son"* (John 5:22).

To the Father	To the Son
Ecc 12:16. *For God will bring every act to judgment, everything which is hidden, whether it is good or evil.* Ecc 11:9. *God will bring you into judgment.*	John 5:27. *He gave Him authority to execute judgment, because He is the Son of Man.* Acts 17:31. *Because he has fixed a day on which he will judge the world in righteousness by a man whom he has appointed; and of this he has given assurance to all by raising him from the dead.*

---

[55] Ridderus, *The Faith and Morality of the Gentiles* (Amsterdam: 1670), 54. This refers to Franciscus Ridderus (1618-1683), a Dutch Reformed minister who served at Schermorhorn, Brielle, and Rotterdam. He wrote religious poems and devotional books.

Gen 18:25. *Shall not the Judge of all the earth do what is just?*[56]	1Co 5:10. *For we must all appear before the judgment seat of Christ, so that each one may receive what is due for what he has done in the body, whether good or evil.*

Now if we examine the texts of the Old Testament and compare them with those of the New, we will find the descriptions of this Judge described the same way.

Ps 50:1. The Judge is called *El Elohim*, Jehovah, the God of Gods, the Lord, or as our version reads, *"the mighty God, even the Lord;"* or as the other translation, *"the Lord, even the most mighty God."* In Ps 96:13 and Ps 98:9 we find that it is Jehovah, the Lord, who *"comes to judge the earth. He will judge the world in righteousness, and the peoples in faithfulness."*

Now from the New Testament we learn that the Father judges no man but has committed all judgment to the Son (John 5:22), and that Christ is the Judge. So, it necessarily follows that Christ the Judge is both God and Man; that Christ the Judge is Jehovah, the God of Gods, the mighty God who comes to judge the earth.

Jesus Christ the Supreme God.

Having thus far seen that all the high titles, all the divine attributes, and all the divine works which are

---

[56] Technically, this verse refers to the Son, as Abraham is having a conversation with the Angel of the LORD.

ascribed to God the Father are ascribed to Christ the Son of God also, we must conclude that this Christ is the very God, the one supreme God with the Father, whose glory is equal, whose majesty is co-eternal.

Every title, every attribute, every work proclaims Christ to be God. All these together make it so clear, so full, so irrefutable a demonstration of his divinity, that one may justly wonder how any who retain the least regard to the Scriptures ever doubt it.

For if these names, attributes, and operations are God's prerogative, and God is by them made known to us, and God is by them distinguished from us; and we have no other criteria to know the divine Nature than by these; we must conclude that wherever these are found, there we find God; and where these are not found, God is not there.

Therefore, if these attributes declare God, we must declare Jesus Christ to be God. For they are all found in him and ascribed to him. If these criteria are not conclusive in regard to Christ, notwithstanding they are found in him, then they cannot be conclusive in any other person, not even for the Father, for we have no other criteria given to us with which we can know the only true God than these. If these are not sufficient for the one, they cannot be for the other; and if they are conclusive for one, they must also be for the other.

To pretend that they are given to the Father in a more eminent manner[57] than to the Son is false and frivolous. Where do they think they have come up with that distinction, and where is it found? They are given exactly alike, and in the most solemn and majestic manner to the Son as they are to the Father. Our adversaries will be eternally at a loss to discover a difference. For instance, in John 1:1, the Word is called God in the same verse as the Father is called God. Should not every man believe that it is to be understood in the same strict and proper sense for two? How shall any judicious reader ever be able to understand language if, in the same verse and same sentence, the same word should stand for two ideas or bear two senses so vastly different from each other? What could move any one in reading this verse to understand one as the true God and the other an inferior God, which is a contradiction in terms? When all the circumstances of the context give us no suspicion of any such different meaning, but the whole thing tends to confirm us that the Word is to be understood in the strict sense to the true God, that is to both, then on what basis does anyone disagree?

The Socinians were at least sensible to the force of the names and attributes of God that to evade it rather than acknowledge Christ to be God, they pretend that the attributes of God are no criteria of the divine

---

[57] Clarke, *Modest Plea*, 148.

Nature. They deny that these attributes are such perfections of the Divinity, as we declare them to be. But, they say they are rather something different from God, something between God and a creature (see Adam Goslavius[58] and others). For them, the divine attributes are something, some third thing between God and the creature, the faculties of God, and the powers of God. They say it is impossible that God can be the attribute "eternity;" eternity cannot be God himself. But is this not a total distraction? Oh, when men are wise beyond revelation, how does God give them up to a reprobate mind! When men willfully depart from the right way, what amazing folly and madness do they run into![59]

But no more of this. I shall only observe that it is a peculiar providence of God that he has bestowed to us so many numbers of evidences for the proof of our Lord's Divinity that less of them would have sufficed. But divine Wisdom, foreseeing what opposition the Gospel of "*God manifest in the flesh*" would meet with,

---

[58] Adam Goslavius was a 17th century Socinian pupil of Nicholas Taurelli. He was a Polish Knight from Bebeln, Germany and had a brother named Andrew who was also a Socinian. De Gols cites here his work *Against Kecherman*, p. 71. In a moment he will cite another Socinian, Jonas Schlichtingius (b. 1592), *Against Meisner*, 12.

[59] There is some deep philosophy going on here. Traditionally, the Church has stated that God "simple." This means that he is indivisible and is not made up of different attributes. Thus, he is not the sum of his attributes, but each attribute simply is what God is. De Gols is affirming this ancient distinction but is not pressing it other than to say that the Socinians were playing with philosophical doctrines surrounding the attributes of God in order to deny that Jesus Christ is God!

purposely guarded it by giving us so many, these great and powerful arguments, so that were it possible for some single evidence by the craft of the Devil to be eluded, the power of the whole would never be overcome.

God's providence is most distinguished in this, because the consequence is so very great. For God would never have brought so many concurring testimonies of a creature's dignity to rob himself of his honor and to deceive the world. For if we are deceived in this article of Faith, it is not man but God who has deceived us. But this is not reconcilable to eternal justice, truthfulness, and goodness. So God, for the honor of his own eternal Son, took all this care and pains to convince us of his Divinity, and furnished us with so many excellent arguments that plead in his behalf, that we might *"honor the Son, even as we honor the Father"* (John 5:23).

Accordingly, all the churches of God in all the dispensations, in all ages of the world, whether Patriarchal, Jewish, or Christian were trained up in the knowledge of the Son of God to know him as the God of their salvation, though in different degrees by those very criteria that are here given of the Divinity of Christ. Truly, upon full consideration we may believe that all mankind would deem it the highest blasphemy to ascribe these lofty titles, these sublime attributes, these almighty works to any created being, which are the only characteristics whereby the Nature of the one only and true God can be made known to us.

And yet we find that from the very age that Christ himself lived, all Christians have ascribed them to Christ, and have stoutly defended them against the heretics in every age. They have accordingly adored and worshiped Christ as the eternal God, the only one and God, to whom all honor and veneration is due.

These evidences, which the holy Scriptures have given us in words as plain and intelligible as could ever possibly be expressed, have had such powerful influence upon men's minds—and not the unthinking part of mankind, but on the most learned,[60] judicious, prudent, and scrupulous, the wisest, and most considerate—that they were forced to embrace the evidence of truth and stooped down with joy and gladness to give glory to the Son of God and to adore God in the Trinity of Persons, in the Unity of the divine Majesty, and worshiped the Father, Son, and Holy Ghost, as the one and only God.

---

[60] De Gols cites Grotius, *de Veritat. Rel. Char.* 1.2. §.3.4.

CHAP. VI.

PRECEPTS OF THE SCRIPTURE THAT ENJOIN US TO WORSHIP CHRIST AS GOD.

Perhaps it will be said, that all that I have said to this point is nothing to the point; that this is neither commanded nor shown by example. I come therefore now to show you both command and example; and shall give you enough of both to convince any man.

But what I have thus far proved concerning the Divinity of Christ was very much to the point, that point being the very foundation, ground, and reason of adoration. For we do not have a god who is a creature, a god made in time, a god of yesterday, a nominal god such as Socinus and most of his followers worship. We worship the true God, and glory in the truth that we do not have a created being, but the eternal God for the object of our worship and adoration.

But before I come to particulars, I must observe that we in our adoration worship the Triune God, the three Persons in the unity of the divine majesty, not excluding but always including the Son and Holy Spirit. And though we sometimes, no and often, pray to God the Father only, without praying directly to the Son or Spirit, we do not therefore exclude them. Rather, we pray this way because the Father is the frontal Divinity, and because we are directed to pray even this way by his Son.

Divines observe that the word "God" is sometimes used "essentially" (*ousiōdōs*, that is, of the essence), and then the three Persons—Father, Son, and Holy Ghost are included and invoked. Whenever the word "God" is used with particular reference to the Father, or Son, or Spirit, this is expressed "personally" (*hupasatikos*, of the persons). For example, Matt 4:7, "*You shall not tempt the Lord your God*," and vs. 10, "*You shall worship the Lord your God*," and John 4:24, "*God is a Spirit.*" In these and other places the word is taken essentially, for the Father, Son, and Holy Ghost, three Persons in the unity of the divine Nature. It is used personally, in places like John 14:1. "*You believe in God*," for the Father; 1Ti 3:16, "*God is manifest in the flesh*," for the Son; Acts 5:4, "*You have lied to God*," for the Holy Ghost, as it is explained in vs. 3.

The same is observed of the word Father also, that it is essentially used for God, who is called the Father of spirits (Heb 12:9), and the Father of all (1Co 8:6); and the Gentiles used to call God by the name of Father. But by the revelation God has given us of his own Nature, that word Father so essentially used, includes all the three Persons, the Father, Son, and Holy Ghost. And so, God is "*our Father*" (Matt 6:4) and "*our heavenly Father*" (Matt 5:16). And so, it is also used personally for the first Person of the sacred Trinity, "The

Father," in a hundred places of Scripture. Yet, is it used of the Son also in Isaiah 9:6, "*The everlasting Father*," where, under correction, the Hebrew signifies the Father of Eternity, and so Junius and Tremellius[61] render it, and the marginal notes of our old version have it, "the Author of Eternity;" and the last Belgic version, and the French.[62]

But that we may pray to the Son of God Christ Jesus, and to the Holy Spirit directly, we have not only warrants from examples in Scripture, but we are commanded so to do. These injunctions will appear as bright as the sun in full glory. For there is no act of adoration so exalted, nor supplication so low, nor veneration so high, nor honor, glory, praise, thanksgiving, or obedience, required of us to be paid to the Father, but what is also required of us, in words of equal weight, and by equal strength of expression, to be paid to Christ the Son of God.

I come now to particulars. The first command is of:

Faith and Reliance.

I begin with this first, because St. Paul has laid it as the foundation of all worship and the principal

---

[61] The Junius-Tremellius Bible (1575). Immanuel Tremellius (1510-80) was an Italian Jewish convert to Christianity, a leading Hebraist and Bible translator. Franciscus Junius was his son-in-law and together they worked on a Latin translation of the Bible from the Hebrew and Syriac.
[62] Of 1618. *Vader der eeuwighent*; *Pere d'Eternite*.

article of adoration (Heb 11:6). *"For without Faith it is impossible to please him; for he that comes to God must believe that he is, and that he is a rewarder of those that diligently seek him."* This faith and reliance, which we are bound to have in the Father, we are by the same Scriptures required to have in the Son.

In the Father	In the Son
John 17:3. *And this is eternal life, that they know you, the only true God.*	John 17:3. *And this is eternal life, that they know you, the only true God, and Jesus Christ whom you have sent.*
John 14:1. *Let not your hearts be troubled. Believe in God.*	John 14:1. *Let not your hearts be troubled. Believe in God; believe also in me.*

Here I must observe, if there is any extraordinary strength or singular significance in the expression of *believing in*, as St. Augustine, the schoolmen after him, and several eminent protestants assert, then it is the highest and most excellent act or degree of faith. The *"full assurance"* (*plērophoria*) of the understanding, which St. Paul speaks of Col 2:2, is the highest thing a Christian grasps in this present life. I say, if there is any strength in that expression, which, however, I dare not say,[63] but if there is, then it is here equally used of the Son as of the Father. But whether there is or is not anything extraordinary in the form of words, I am very

---

[63] De Gols cites Peter Haylin (1599-1662) on the Apostle's Creed here.

sure there is in the duty required. That is, namely, that whatever faith, reliance, hope, trust, or confidence we are to exercise in God by virtue of God's excellencies and his dominion over us, we are to put the same faith, reliance, hope, trust, and confidence in the Lord Jesus, because of his divine excellencies and his dominion over us as God, and our Redeemer.

We should consider Jer 17:7, *"Blessed is the Man that trusts in the Lord, whose trust is the LORD;"* and on the contrary, *"Cursed is the man who trusts in man and makes flesh his strength, whose heart turns away from the LORD"* (vs. 5). When we duly weigh this and compare it with the text of St. John, who requires our faith and reliance in Jesus Christ equally as in the Father, must we not conclude that Jesus is the same God with the Father, or that his gospel draws us away from God and exposes us to the direst curses?

But as we know that the end of the gospel is to bring us to God, and speaks peace to believers, so we are assured that this Jesus in whom we must believe equally as in the Father, is God, is the Son of God, of the same divine nature with the Father, whose glory is equal, whose majesty is co-eternal. And we are further assured by the same Scriptures that God the Father, for the highest demonstration of his love towards us, has given us this very Jesus, that we might believe in him and be happy through by faith. I am sure our Saviour says so. John 3:16, *"For God so loved the world that he gave his only begotten Son, that whosoever believes in him should not perish but have everlasting life. For God did not send his Son into the world to condemn the world, but in order that the world might be saved through him."* It is very remarkable that St. John, who wrote his Gospel purposely to vindicate and prove the divinity of Christ more than the other Evangelists, insists on this duty of believing in him in a very extraordinary manner. As John 3:36 says, *"Whoever believes in the Son has eternal life; whoever does not obey the Son shall not see life, but the wrath of God remains on him."* Or John 6:29, *"This is the work of God, that you believe in him whom he has sent"* (cf. John 6:35, 43, 47; 9:35, 36, 38; 20:31, etc.). For of this Christ it says, *"to him all the prophets bear witness that everyone who believes in him receives forgiveness of sins through his name"* (Acts 10:43). From these and many more places in the New Testament, we have a sufficient warrant and command for believing in Christ, which is the principle part of worship and adoration.

Yes, the Scriptures prove that believing in Christ is actually believing in God; for when Paul and Silas had exhorted the keeper of the prison *"to believe on the Lord Jesus Christ"* (Acts 16:31), it is said, *"That when he was baptized he rejoiced, believing in God with all his house"* (34).

The second precept is, to love God.

This duty God requires of us as our God, Creator and Benefactor; and also for our own sakes, that our love of God may return with a blessing back to us. The Scripture requires this duty of us as part of that worship we owe God, and it requires it equally to the Son of God as to God the Father.

To the Father	To the Son
Deut 6:5. *You shall love the LORD your God with all your heart and with all your soul and with all your might.*	Mat 10:37. *Whoever loves father or mother more than me is not worthy of me.*
Jdg 5:31. *Let all your enemies perish, O Lord, but let them that love him be as when the sun goes forth in his might* (NKJV).	John 8:42. *If God were your Father, you would love me, for I came from God and I am here. I came not of my own accord, but he sent me.*
Ps 5:11. *That those who love your Name may exult in you.*	1Pe 1:8. *Though you have not seen him, you love him. Though you do not now see him, you believe in him and rejoice with joy that is inexpressible and filled with glory.*
Matt 22:37. *You shall love the Lord your God with all your heart and with all your soul and with all your mind.*	Eph 6:24. *Grace be with all who love our Lord Jesus Christ with love incorruptible.*
	1Co 16:22. *If anyone has no love for the Lord, let him be accursed. Our Lord, come!*

Now if any man will consider and compare these texts, he will see that the duty of loving Christ is not only enjoined, but is enforced with a benediction to the obedient and with the penalty of a dreadful curse to the disobedient.

Anathema Maranatha (*Cursed. Our Lord, come*). Our English version of [Geneva Bible] 1599, reads this verse, "*Let him be had in execration, maranatha.*" The margin note explains it,

> By these words is betokened the severest kind of curse and excommunication that was amongst the Jews; and the words are as much as to say, as "our Lord cometh": So that his meaning may be this, Let him be accursed even to the coming of the Lord, that is to say, to his death's day, even forever.

The first word, "anathema," signifies an eternal curse, condemnation, or being doomed to destruction. It is used this way in Rom 1:9; Gal 1:8, 9. The other word, "maranatha," whether Syrian[64] or Chaldean, which signifies the Lord's Coming, is added to show that the doom is certain, that the Lord will come to confirm the condemnation. This imprecation therefore is the highest that words are able to express; in the same manner as the duty is enforced by the highest blessing that can be conceived, "*If any Man love me, he will keep my words, and my Father will love him, and we will come to him, and make our dwelling with him*" (John 14:23).

---

[64] De Gols cites Ravanel, *Bibliotheca*, vol. 2, p. 35 here.

Thirdly, Another Precept is, to Honor God.

That honor is due to God is a principle of natural as well as revealed religion. Hence God expostulates with the Jews, through the Prophet Malachi, "*A son honors his father, and a servant his master. If then I am a father, where is my honor? And if I am a master, where is my fear? says the LORD of hosts*" (Mal 1:6).

The duty therefore of honoring God is required of us in the holy Scriptures in the most express terms; and the same honor which is to be paid to the Father, is also required to be paid to the Son, in terms equally strong, and by motives equally cogent.

To the Father	**To the Son**
Ps 86:9-10, 12. *All the nations you have made shall come and worship before you, O Lord, and shall glorify your name. For you are great and do wondrous things; you alone are God … I give thanks to you, O Lord my God, with my whole heart, and I will glorify your name forever.*	John 5:23. *That all may honor the Son, just as they honor the Father. Whoever does not honor the Son does not honor the Father who sent him.*
Ps 96:7-8. *Ascribe to the LORD, O families of the peoples, ascribe to the LORD glory and strength! Ascribe to*	Rev 5:12. *Worthy is the Lamb who was slain, to receive power and wealth and wisdom and might and honor and glory and blessing!* Php 2:10-11. *That at the name of Jesus every knee should bow, in heaven and on earth and under the earth, and every tongue*

the LORD the glory due his name.

confess that Jesus Christ is Lord, to the glory of God the Father.

Here I must take leave to consider a little more particularly that last admirable citation of St. Paul to the Philippians, where the Apostle sets forth the great condescension of Christ, and the glory that ensued, and the duty required of us to honor the Lord Christ.

The condescension is all the greater because of the state of honor which the Lord Christ had before, which was nothing less than divine glory; for he was in the form of God (*en morphē Theou*), such a one as God is, that is, the true God, or truly God.[65] This expression is only found in this place and is illustrated by what follows, to be equal with God; and that without robbery or prejudice to the divine Majesty. St. Paul explains this in Col 1:15 by being the image of the invisible God, and by being born before the very creation; that is, that he was the eternal Son with the eternal Father, eternal God.

And yet he humbled himself, a humiliation which has several gradations. *He made himself of no reputation; he took upon him the form of a servant; he was made in the likeness of men, and being in fashion as a man, he humbled himself and became obedient unto death, even the death of the cross.* And here it is to be observed, that the Apostle expresses the *form of a servant, and the likeness of men,*

---

[65] Beza, in loc.

in opposition to the other expression of *the form of God*; that he was as truly God, as he was truly man.

When Christ is said to have made himself of *no reputation*, or when *he emptied himself* or *divested himself*, we must not suppose that he lost anything which he had before, or that he was no more in the *form of God* because he had taken upon him the *form of man*. No, he still retained the same essential glory, the same divine dignity, which he always had. But he concealed it for a time. He did appear among men in the brightness of his divine nature, but laid aside his glory, and divested himself of his splendor, and appeared in our nature as a miserable man, as a *man of sorrows*, to become the sacrifice for our sins.

Then follows the exaltation, *wherefore God also has highly exalted him*. This was an exaltation as high as his humiliation was low; and therefore the Apostle expressly says, *highly exalted him*. The Word in the original is *huperupsen*, raised to the highest degree of glory; which the Psalmist expresses in these words, *For you, O LORD, are most high over all the earth; you are exalted far above all gods* (Ps 97:9).

But how was Christ capable of such an exaltation if he was already God? Can the divine nature be exalted, or can infinity receive a further degree of glory? Some therefore explain this exaltation as pertaining to the human nature of Christ, and very rightly: for the divine nature cannot be exalted. He that was God before the worlds were made could not receive an addition of greatness; *from everlasting to everlasting you are God*: He that was adored by angels and men before his incarnation could not receive a new privilege of worship. And therefore, this exaltation is a new investiture upon his late condescension, a recognition of his rights and privileges which he had from eternity as God, but has now as *Theanthropos*—God and man.

Because Christ, who is the eternal God, condescended so low as to die on a cross for man's redemption, it was fitting that God the Father should declare that it was he who made atonement and paid the price of redemption. It was fitting moreover that the Father should declare that this Redeemer was none less than the very Son of God, that he was now set before the world as their God and their Lord, and that all men might honor him as such, as their God and as their Lord; that they might honor him as their God always, but now as their Lord, their Redeemer by a new claim and a new title.

For this title as Savior was certainly new; for although Christ was ever blessed in his divine nature and perfections, yet had he remained so, and not become our Savior by taking our nature upon him and dying for our sins, he could never have received that title of Savior. For that was subsequent to his sufferings, according to what St. Paul says in Heb 2:9: *But we see Jesus, who was made a little lower than the angels, for the suffering of death, crowned with glory and honor.* And St. Peter in Acts 2:36: *Therefore, let all the house of Israel know assuredly, that God has made that same Jesus whom you have crucified, both Lord and Christ.*

This exaltation is declaring and proclaiming the excellency of this great Person—who he is, and what he is, namely, God eternal. It tells us that he has become the author of salvation and that all must obey him. St. Paul tells us that this exaltation consisted in giving him a *Name above every name*; that is, declaring his divine nature, that he is the eternal God. That the Word "exalting" will bear this meaning is plain from Psalm 128:28, *You are my God, and I will give thanks to you; you are my God; I will extol you*; and from Psalm 18:46, *The LORD lives, and blessed be my rock, and exalted be the God of my salvation.*

For what end was this declaration of the transcendent excellency of the Lord Jesus? This the Apostle tells us, *that at the name of Jesus every knee should bow, in heaven and on earth and under the earth, and every tongue confess that Jesus Christ is Lord, to the glory of God the Father* (Php 2:10-11).

Is this not a precept? Is this not a command? Is this not an injunction for worshiping Christ as God, he who is in the *form of God*, who is *equal with God*, and that *without robbing* God of divine glory? If this is not a precept, no words can express any. No words can more fully express a command than to tell us that the whole design of this exaltation and declaration of his divine nature was that all rational creatures should adore him, that all men should worship him as God and Savior, whether moved by fear or by love.

This worship we are to pay to Christ, to the glory of God the Father. The Apostle has added this on purpose, so that we, while admiring the greatness of the Son, should not forget the Father whose Son he is. Rather, he did it so that we should glorify the Father who has created us, and the Son who has redeemed us with his blood, and to whom, with the Holy Spirit the One God might be all honor and glory for ever and ever. Amen.

Another Duty is, To serve and obey God

God is the Sovereign Lord of the world. He has a right to our service and may command our obedience. The Scriptures require our service and obedience under the highest penalty, even of eternal damnation.

This service and obedience is in and by the same Scriptures required to be paid to the Lord Christ, God the Son, as it is to God the Father.

To the Father	To the Son
Dt 13:4. *You shall walk after the LORD your God and fear him and*	Ex 23:20-22. *Behold, I send an angel before you to guard you on the way ... Pay careful attention to him and obey his voice; do not rebel against him, for he will*

keep his commandments and obey his voice, and you shall serve him and hold fast to him. Dt 27:10. *You shall therefore obey the voice of the LORD your God, keeping his commandments.*

not pardon your transgression, for my name is in him. But if you carefully obey his voice and do all that I say, then I will be an enemy to your enemies and an adversary to your adversaries. Matt 17:5. *This is my beloved Son, with whom I am well pleased; listen to him.* John 12:26. *If anyone serves me, he must follow me; and where I am, there will my servant be also. If anyone serves me, the Father will honor him.*

It would never end if we were to quote all the texts of the New Testament which require our obedience to Christ. We may only observe the gracious manner of these injunctions. They are not in the harsh terms of a lawgiver, not in the severe dictates of a judge, but in the terms of love and with the motives of our own happiness. But though the terms are gentler, the duty is the same; and indeed the obligation from the grace and goodness of God ties us down all the more to the duty.

The inanimate part of the world obeys Christ; the *very wind and the sea obey him* (Matt 8:27). Nay, the very devils are forced to obey him (Mark 1:27). How much more are we obliged to serve him, whose service is perfect freedom, him who is our God and Savior, him who proposes his laws to us in the strains of mercy and of love!

Christ *the Object of Love, not of Fear*

I know it is objected that there is no precept to fear him. But that is easily accounted for, because Christ is proposed to us as the object of our love and not our fear; as our Saviour, our Redeemer; not primarily as our Judge, and therefore not the object of fear, but of love, hope, joy, and consolation. Though I am very sure that they who do not love him have the greatest reason in the world to fear him; but those that love and obey him, fear him with a reverential fear, though they dread him not. *For you have not received the Spirit of bondage again to fear; but you have received the Spirit of Adoption, whereby we cry, Abba, Father* (Rom 8:15).

Those who neglect the soft voice of love and mercy and peace, will find the day of his Second Coming terrible enough and will have reason to fear him, *when the Lord Jesus is revealed from heaven with his mighty angels in flaming fire, inflicting vengeance on those who do not know God and on those who do not obey the gospel of our Lord Jesus. They will suffer the punishment of eternal destruction, away from the presence of the Lord and from the glory of his might, when he comes on that day to be glorified in his saints, and to be marveled at among all who have believed, because our testimony to you was believed* (2Th 1:7-10; cf. Rev 1:7; 6:15-17).

Another duty required by positive precept is,
To pray to God.

Prayer and supplication are certainly the principal acts of divine worship, and God requires them from us. When we do them, we acknowledge him to be the Fountain of all good, and own our continual dependency upon his favor.

That this duty of prayer was not known nor required in the Old Testament is Socinus's opinion, who says it is an additional precept of Christ to the First Commandment. Smalcius[66] is of the same opinion, that prayer was not required by Almighty God in the Old Testament. As to the worshiping of Christ, this they allow also to be an additional precept of Christ to the First Commandment. But how? Christ has enjoined us that we are to acknowledge him as God (that is, for such a one that has divine power over us) and to pay him religious worship, as the Racovian Catechism expresses it.[67]

This is strange, that Christ should enjoin this, that this should be the peculiar precept of Christ, and yet there should be no precept of worshiping Christ anywhere found in the Scriptures, as Socinus claims, and Staunton from him.

---

[66] Valentinus Smalcius (1572-1622) was a German Socinian. DeGols gives locations and Latin quotes for both men.
[67] This is Socinius' catechism.

How inconsistent are these men with themselves, at one time to assert, at another time to deny what they asserted before! But in answer to their proportions:

First, it is entirely false that the duty of prayer was never commanded in the Old Testament. For in Dt 6:5 we find, *You shall love the Lord your God with all your heart, and with all your soul, and with all your might,* which cannot be done without prayer and adoration; and Vs. 13. *You shall fear the Lord your God and serve him, and shall swear by his Name* which cannot be done without invocation. What is the meaning of this precept in Ps 50:15? *Call upon me in the day of trouble;* or in Isa 55:6, *Seek the Lord while he may be found, call upon him while he is near;* or in Isa 56:7, *My house shall be called a house of prayer for all people?*

The examples of people praying, and the prayers recorded, are so frequent that I need not name them.

As to a form of prayer, there never was any age of the church without a form: Before the Flood, as soon as the sons of God had separated themselves from the sons of men,[68] they had a form of worship, certain rites, certain sacrifices, and certain prayers; and no doubt but the prayers were equally revealed as the sacrifices were. It appears from the Epistle of Jude that there was even in his time some remains of the

---

[68] De Gols takes "sons of God" here in the traditional Reformed-Augustinian interpretation to mean godly men as opposed to the "sons of men" who were ungodly men.

antediluvian [pre-Flood] liturgy called the Book of Enoch.[69] This book contained the prayers of the first world, as Tertullian (*habit. Mulier.*) and Augustine (*City of God*) thought. The Jews are of opinion that several of the Psalms were composed before the Flood and reserved for the use of the Jewish Church.

After the Flood, we find a Prayer of Abraham (Gen 18:27), the Liturgy of Isaac (Gen 32:9), and the form of Moses (Ex 34:9), all which are recorded, not only to assure us that God is the God of order in all the churches, but to confront those men who, with falsehood and lies, go about to deceive.

As soon as God had given the Jews his laws as the form of obedience, he gave them also a form of prayer (Ex 34:9; Num 6:24); and we find that Moses used it, and it was used by the kings of Israel many years after (1Kg 8; Ezra 9). The prophets composed forms of prayer suitable to particular occasions; as the prayer for the Sabbath (Ps 92), the prayer for the Feast of Tabernacles (Ps 98), and that it was used on the festival we find in Ezra 3:11, the prayer for the sick (Ps 102), and the Psalms of Degrees were the daily form of common prayer throughout the year. And the Jews tell us, and it appears also from Jeremiah 32, Habakkuk 3, Joel 2 and other of the prophets, that they had peculiar forms of prayer when in captivity, in war, or in times of

---

[69] Since DeGol's time, the book of Enoch has been rediscovered.

pestilence, or famine; and Agur's prayer seems to have been composed for daily devotion (Prov 30:7).

After the Prophets, John the Baptist taught the Jews another form of prayer, which although it is not in existence today, we believe was in the name of the Messiah, not to come, as the prophets (Dan 9:17), but as already come.

And when Christ the eternal Son of God came, and gave us his most excellent form, he had no misgivings about collecting the petitions out of the several forms of prayer, then in use among the Jews.

So much in answer to the first proposition, which the Socinians borrowed from the ancient Manichees who held that Christ made Prayer an addition to the First Commandment; and that Prayer was not known to the Fathers, nor required under the Mosaic dispensation. But that this is most notoriously false, appears from what has been said.

As to the second proposition, that the worship of Christ is an additional precept to the First Commandment, a precept added by Jesus Christ himself; how this can be reconciled to the assertion and positive expression of Socinus and of Mr. Staunton from him, that there is neither command nor example to worship Christ as God. I cannot tell, nor do I believe any man living can resolve this. Both cannot be true, that's certain; and that there is neither command nor example, I have in part and shall further prove the contrary.

If it were true, that Christ added to the law for his own worship, that would be no addition to the law, but a total destruction of the law. There could be nothing more contrary to the law. For the First Commandment is, *You shall have no other gods before me.* This forbids every kind of divine worship that could be paid to any being whatsoever, except God. Therefore, to make a created being to be God, exalting him to the highest degree of honor, and giving divine adoration to him, if that is not contrary to and a violation of the First Commandment, then that commandment cannot be violated.

As a matter of fact, that Christ was worshiped in the Old Testament and that there are commands relating to his worship, nothing is plainer: Psalm 2:12 *Kiss the Son*; Psalm 45:11 *Since he is your Lord, bow to him.* Daniel prayed for the Lord's sake (Dan 9:17) and all the Jews prayed for the mediation of the Messiah, for which reason they prayed towards the temple and towards the Ark of the Covenant—the type and figure of Christ, This is beyond all doubt, and that Christ was worshiped in the Old Testament, and before, as well as in the New, I shall now show.

For a plain and positive precept for worshiping Christ as God, nothing can be more plain and positive than Rom 10:13. *Everyone who calls on the name of the Lord will be saved.*

And that this was spoken of Christ appears from the context, for no other person but Christ is mentioned. For at the 4th verse, Christ is called the end of the law, and at the 12th verse he is Lord over all. The necessity of believing in and confessing him is urged at the 9th verse, *If you confess with your mouth that Jesus is Lord and believe in your heart that God raised him from the dead, you will be saved.* Importantly, the Apostle, in citing several texts out of the Old Testament, does not signify that person to be anyone other than Christ. Instead, he fully demonstrates that this Christ was known and called upon by the Fathers of the Old Testament. The duty of calling upon Christ in this text, is commanded not simply, but under a penalty nothing less than damnation.

What must we think therefore of such men as dare openly declare the contrary? What front must we suppose them to have, to impose upon the world such notorious falsehoods? Is there no precept to worship Christ as God? Are faith, love, honor, service, and invocation not worship? Why then what is worship? Of what does divine worship consist, if not in these duties? What peculiar worship does the Scripture ascribe to the only one God, which it does not ascribe and require us to pay to the Lord Jesus Christ? No, I dare be so bold as to challenge any Socinian or Anti-trinitarian, any enemy to Christ, to show me any act of worship, or homage, or adoration, or obedience which is to be paid to the supreme God, which is not by the Scriptures also given to Jesus Christ and required of us by positive precept to be paid to the Lord Christ.

That Christ was worshiped as God, their great master Socinus has more than once acknowledged; and either that, or the fear of the civil power, moved him to do the same, whatever he taught others, or denied before. What must we think of these men? Are they judicially blinded that they cannot see, or are they willfully blind that they will not understand? Either is dreadful. I would have them remember that those who first refuse to know and worship Christ, may afterwards be given over to a reprobate mind and judicially hardened. It is justice for God to withdraw his light and grace which men have abused, and which they have applied to affront and dishonor their God and Saviour.

CHAP. VII

CHRIST ADORED AS GOD, BY INSTANCES IN THE SCRIPTURE

I come now to the matter where I shall demonstrate that the Lord Jesus Christ has been adored and worshiped as God, as the true and eternal God, by numerous instances recorded in the Scriptures.

Christ adored as God by the Angels.

St. Paul assures us that all the angels of God worshiped him at his incarnation. *When he brings the firstborn into the world, he says, "Let all God's angels worship him"* (Heb 1:6; Dt 32:43 LXX).

David tells us that the Angels of God worshiped him before his incarnation, *Worship him all you gods* (Ps 97:7), which the Septuagint has rendered *worship him all his angels*; for the Hebrew *elohim*, "gods," is a name sometimes given to angels because of their exalted strength and power.[70] They are called upon in that Psalm, which is a prophecy of the kingdom of Christ the Messiah, to worship and adore him. If this worship had not been paid by the angels to Christ, the Apostle could not have produced that psalm for the proof of

---

[70] DeGols cites Buxtorf. *Lex.*, p. 29.

it; but from that allegation it is evident that the gods, or angels, worshiped Christ as well before as at his incarnation.

Jesus Christ worshiped as God by Men.

As Christ was worshiped by the angels, so he was likewise worshiped by the sons of men as their God, as the only true and eternal God. The Scriptures are as clear in this as words can express or demonstrate.

Christ was worshiped as God in every Dispensation, by Adam, by the Antediluvian Fathers, by Noah in the Ark, by the Patriarchs, by Moses and Joshua, by the Israelites in the wilderness, by David and the prophets, by the Apostles and Christians to this very time. The matter of fact of this adoration is recorded with so much care, caution, and concern, that after all, if God the Son was not worshiped equally with the Father as God, we must conclude that then neither has God the Father been worshiped from the creation of the world to this day.

But before I proceed, I must lay down this axiom, that God the Father in all the appearances God was pleased to make to mankind, never appeared visible himself, but always by the *Memra (mmr')*, that is, the *Word*, as St. John expressly calls him (John 1:1). This is according to what is said in Exodus 33:20, *You cannot see my face, for man shall not see me and live*; and to what our Saviour says, that *no man hath seen the Father* (John 6:46) and *His voice you have never heard, his form you have never seen* (5:37). Every revelation of God is through Christ his Son, who is the revealer and interpreter of the otherwise unknown Father, and his will to men. This order and economy in the Persons of the sacred Trinity is what we ought humbly to adore and reverence, rather than pry too curiously into. We must not pretend to be wise above what is written, lest we fall into errors and lose ourselves in inextricable mazes. For to say (Eusebius, *Demonstration of the Gospel*) that the *to theion*, the frontal Divinity, became visible, is extreme erroneous, *for no man has seen God at any time, the only begotten Son, which is in the bosom of the Father, he has made him known* (John 1:18).

The Logos, or Word, explained.

Because our adversaries have with a world of art endeavored to perplex and entangle men's minds, about the true meaning of the *Logos*, or Word, I shall give a clear explication of the phrase and show,

> That it was a term and expression to signify a Divine Person, both by Jews and Gentiles; and that it was used long before and after the age that St. John wrote his Gospel; and that it was that very expression whereby the Jews understood the Messiah.

The Word, or Logos, taken by the Jews for a Divine Person.

As for the Jews, how and in what sense they used it is evident from the Septuagint, and Philo, and the Chaldee paraphrase (i.e. the Targums) namely, for a Divine Person. For example, in Ezek 1:24, the LXX has changed *Shaddai*, the undoubted Name of the omnipotent God, into *logos*, the Word. This they would never have done had they not thought this Word a divine Person.

Philo the Jew, who lived in the age St. John wrote his Gospel, expressly calls this Word *deutron theon*, the Second God, next to the "Father of all things." Elsewhere he wrote that the Word is superior to the whole World and more ancient and general than anything that is made. Again, speaking of the world's being the temple of God, he says, in this temple the High Priest is the Firstborn Divine Word of God. In another book he says this Divine Word is superior to all things; it has no visible species by which it may be likened to any sensible thing, but is itself the Image of God, the most ancient of all intelligibles, and next to the most High, between whom and him there is no medium.

Grotius says, that Philo taught that the Word of God is the Maker of the world, not unbegotten as is God the Father of all, nor yet begotten in like manner as men are. And again, that the Word of God is the Angel or Ambassador of God, who takes care of the universe. And he further quotes some ancient Cabalists who distinguish God into three Lights, which some of them call by the same names we Christians do: Father, Son or Word, and Holy Ghost.

The Chaldee Paraphrase, which is one of the most ancient monuments of Jewish learning, constantly by the Word signifies a divine Person. For instead of Jehovah or God as we have in the Hebrew text, it commonly has *the Word of Jehovah*. "Word" is attributed with personal actions. Thus, it is evident that they looked upon it as a divine Person. For instance,

The Hebrew Text	**The Targum**
Gen 1:27. *And God made man in his own image.*	Gen 1:27. *And the Word of God made man in his own image.*
Gen 3:8. *And they heard the voice of the Lord.*	Gen 3:8. *And they heard the voice of the Word of the Lord.*
Gen 3:22. *And the Lord God said, "Behold, the man has become like one of us."*	Gen 3:22. *The Word of Jehovah God said, "Behold, Adam whom I created, is the only begotten in the world, even as I am the only begotten in the highest heavens."*[71]

---

[71] De Gols translation here is different from modern translations, which do not have "begotten." His should be considered!

Gen 28:20-21. *If God will be with me ... then shall the Lord be my God.*
Ex 20:1. *And God spoke.*

Gen 28:20-21. *If the Word of the Lord will be with me ... the Word of the Lord shall be my God*
Ex 20:1. *The Word of the Lord God spoke.*

Num 11:20. *You have despised the Lord who is among you.*

Num 11:20. *You have despised the Word of Jehovah, whose divinity dwells among you.*

Dt 1:30, 32. *The Lord your God who goes before you, he shall fight for you ... You did not believe the Lord your God.*

Dt 1:30, 32. *The Word of Jehovah, he shall fight for you ... You did not believe in the Word Jehovah your God.*

Isa 45:17. *Israel is saved by the LORD with everlasting salvation.*

Isa 45:17. *Israel shall be saved by the Word of God with everlasting salvation.*

Those who desire more may consult Rittangel, who had been a Jew, and was well skilled in the Jewish learning.[72] There they may find that Memra is a divine Person, and divine Subsistence, and never used by the Chaldee Paraphrasts otherwise.

Since therefore it is evident that by this Word they meant a person; and since to this person they ascribe not only the name, but the worship of God, it is plain they believed him to be a divine Person.

---

[72] Johann Stephan Rittangel (1602-1652), a German Jew who converted to Roman Catholicism, then became a Calvinist, and later a Lutheran. He was professor of Oriental languages at Königsberg. De Gols cites a work *Jesirah*, p. 96. This is probably *Sefer Yezira* (1642). But he also wrote works called *Bilibra Veritatis* and *Veritas Religionis Christianæ* (1699) to substantiate the claim that the Targums prove the Trinity.

Accordingly, *Chalcidius ad Timæum*, in that book where he professes to explain the doctrines of the Jews, whom he calls the holy sect, delivers this as their sense of this divine Word.

This *Word of God* is God, taking care of human affairs, and is the Cause or Principle by which men may live well and happily, if they do not neglect this gift which the supreme God has granted to them.

And to the same purpose Celsus,[73] speaking the sense of the Jews, expressly tells us, "*We agree with you, that the Word is the Son of God.*"

I come now to see how the Gentiles used it and that they also understood by it a divine Person. What the Gentiles knew of the Trinity is not my present business to examine. What they had, they received from the Hebrews, but so grievously depraved and adulterated that nothing can be made of it but confusion. However, those who desire to know may consult Agrippa, Gale, and others.[74] It is enough for my purpose to know what they understood by Word.

---

[73] Celsus (2nd Cent. AD), Greek philosopher and opponent of Christianity. The work was called *A True Discourse*, but it now lost, known to us through passages preserved by Origen. Someone else quotes Celsus as saying, "We agree with you Jews, that the Word is the Son of God." David Simpson, *A Plea for the Deity of Jesus and the Doctrine of the Trinity* (London, 1812), 448.

[74] Henry Cornelius Agrippa (1486-1535), *Three Books of Occult Philosophy or Magic*, 1.3.c.8; Theophilus Gale (1628-1678), *The Court of the Gentiles*, Part IV. 1.2. This is a point made by Peter Allix. For example, "It is certain, that Plato himself, by conversing with the Jews in Egypt, borrowed of them the best notions he had of God." Peter Allix, *The Judgment of the Ancient Jewish Church Against the Unitarians*, second edition (Oxford: Clarendon Press, 1821), 2. This idea goes back at least as

The Logos or Word, how used by the Gentiles.

Tertullian (*Apologet.* 36) will tell us, Zeno has declared that the Logos, the Word, is a maker of the world, who formed all things in due temper, and is called Fate and God, and the Soul of Jupiter.

Orpheus (see Clement, *Strom.* 1.5) says, that the Word is the divine and immortal King.

Numenius the Pythagorean, as he is quoted by St. Cyril (*Against Julian* 1.8), calls the Father the First, and the Word the Second God. And Plotinus (Enn. 5.1.5.c.3) also, speaking of this divine Mind or Word, says this Nature is God, a Second God.

The Logos, or Word, is the very Expression used by the Jews to signify the Messiah.

That the Jews meant not only a divine Person by the Word, but even the very Messiah whom they looked for is evident, not only because they give him the very same characters which the New Testament gives to our Savior, but also because they attribute to him the very same offices that the New Testament attributes to Christ.

---

far as Justin Martyr. "Plato clearly and openly alludes to the law of Moses, but, fearing the hemlock, he did not dare mention him by name whose teaching, he well knew, was hateful to the Greeks."(Justin Martyr, *Exhortation to the Greeks* 25).

First, the Jews give the Word the same characters the Gospel gives Christ.

Philo says the Word is the "character of God" (*On Agriculture* 1.2) and the "image of God" (possibly *Allegorical Interpretation* or *On Agriculture*); answerable to St. Paul (Heb 1:3): *The express image of his Person.* The bread and food which God has given to the soul; answerable to John 6:33, 35. *I am the Bread of Life.* He says the Word is the house of the Father in which he dwells (*On the Migration of Abraham*), agreeable to John 14:10. *"Do you not believe that I am in the Father and the Father is in me? … but the Father who dwells in me does his works."*

Secondly, The Jews attribute to the Word the same offices that the New Testament ascribes to Christ.

So they say, the Word or divine Logos is the Governor of all things, and the Viceroy of the great King (Philo, *On Dreams* & *On Agriculture* 1.2). They say that God, who is King and Pastor of the world, has appointed the Word, his first-begotten Son, to undertake the care of his sacred flock as his own Viceroy and Substitute (*ibid*). The same Philo has a passage relating to the Word, as the intercessor between God and Man, which is highly worthy of our observation (*ibid*).

> This excellent gift (of Intercessor), the Father of all things has bestowed upon the Prince of Angels, the most ancient Word, that standing in the middle, he might judge between the creature and the Creator. He always supplicates the immortal

God for mortals, and is the ambassador from the supreme King to his subjects. In this gift he rejoices as highly valuing himself upon it, saying, I stood in the middle between you and the Lord, as being neither unbegotten as God, nor yet begotten as you, but am a middle between the extremes, and a pledge for both; for the creature with the Creator, that he shall not wholly apostatize from him, so as to prefer disorder before order and beauty; for the Creator with the creatures, to give him an assured hope that the most merciful God will never abandon his own workmanship. For I declare peace to the creature from him who makes wars to cease, even God, who is the King of Peace.

The same Philo (*The Worse Attacks the Better*) himself understood the Messiah by the Word; for he applied those Words of Ezekiel, which the ancient Jews unanimously understood of the Messiah, to the Word. The Words of Ezekiel are these, *And you shall know that I am the LORD, when their slain lie among their idols around their altars* (Ezek 6:13).

But to put all out of doubt, the Targums use the *Word of the Lord*, and the Messiah promiscuously. For so on those words, *I wait for your salvation, O Lord* (Gen 49:18), the Targum says,

> *Our Father Jacob said, "I expect not the salvation of Gideon, son of Joash, which is a temporal salvation; nor*

the salvation of Samson, son of Manoah, which is a transitory salvation; but I expect the redemption of Messiah, the son of God, who shall come and gather together the sons of Israel; his redemption my soul expects. "[75]

The Jerusalem Targum has almost the same Words, with only this difference, that instead of "*I expect the Redemption of Messiah the Son of David*," it has, "But I expect the Redemption which you have promised to give us by your Word.[76] So also on these Words, "*See now that I, even I, am he, and there is no god beside me; I kill and I make alive; I wound and I heal*" (Dt 32:39); the Targum of Jonathan runs thus, "When the Word of the Lord shall be manifested to redeem his people, he, the Word of the Lord, shall say to all the people, 'See now because I am he, who was, and is, and is to come, and there is no other God beside me; I kill in my revenge, and reviving do revive the people of the house of Israel. I will heal them in the last days." And nothing is more common with the Jews than to call the days of the Messiah the last days.

---

[75] Most translations do not render anything about David. De Gols is getting this from the Neofiti Targum CTg X (a Tosefta) or Cairo Genizah (Pal.) manuscript. See Kevin Cathcart, Michael Maher, and Martin McNamara, eds., *The Aramaic BibleA: Targum Neofiti 1: Genesis*, trans. Martin McNamara, vol. 1 (Collegeville, MN: The Liturgical Press, 1992), Gen 49:18, p. 222, note j.

[76] The Tosefta fragmentary text says: "Their father said to them: Not for the redemption of Gideon bar Joash do I wait, for it is a transient redemption and not for the redemption of Samson bar Manoah, which is a transient redemption, but for the redemption of the King Messiah, which is the eternal redemption which you have promised (lit.: "said") in your Memra to br(ing)."

Having seen that this Word was used both by Jews and Gentiles for a divine Person, and that it was a term whereby the Jews understood the Messiah the Savior; I shall now demonstrate that St. John used the same expression as it had been understood and received both by Jews and Gentiles before, and that he put no new meaning nor different signification upon it, but only such as was already known and received by all men.

But this will better appear by comparing the expressions of St. John and the Jews and Gentiles together.

St. John	Jews and Gentiles
John 1:1. *In the beginning was the Word.*	Porphryr, quoted by St. Cyril (*Against Jul. 1.1*) says that the Logos or Word, is *"always without time, and alone eternal." And the Word of God made man in his own image.* Philo says, he is the most ancient Word of God (*On Dreams*), and the most ancient of all things that are (*Ibid.*, 16; *Allegorical Interpretation 1.2*).
John 1:2. *He was in the beginning with God.*	So the Jews and Gentiles affirm (Plotin. *En.* 5.1.i.c.6), that their Word is not separated from the First Good, or Father, but of necessity is together with him.
John 1:3. *All things were made by him, and without*	All the Platonic schools call the Word the "Artificer of the world" and Plato himself speaking of the world said, "Which world the word, which of all things is the

him was not anything made that was made. most divine, framed and set in order. And Philo calls him, the Instrument by whom God made the world (*On the Cherubim*).

John 1:4. *In him was Life.* Jew and Gentile affirm that their Word is the *to on*, the Being, the Existence, and that this Being is not a dead Being, that is (Plotin, *Enn.* 1.5.c.2) neither Life nor Mind, but is Life, and Mind, and Being itself.

John 1:4. *And the Life was the Light of men.* So they affirm that the Life of their Word was Knowledge and Understanding (Plotin, *Enn.* 1.3.c.5), neither is this Mind or Word *in potentia*, neither is itself one thing, and its Knowledge another, but its Knowledge is itself, or its own Being.

John 1:9. *The true light, which gives light to everyone, was coming into the world.* So they, Jews and Gentiles say, that intelligible Light proceeded from the Word (Philo, *On the Creation of the World*), and that all Light is from this Word or Wisdom (Aristob. in Euseb. *Preparation for the Gospel*).

John 1:14. *The Word … the only begotten of the Father.* The Jews and Gentiles style their Word the Son of God (Plotin, *Enn.* 5.1.8.c.5); and again the Son or child of God, the full beautiful Mind, even the Mind that is full of God (Philo, *l. de perfectiore*); as also the

John 1:18. *The only begotten Son.* most ancient Son of the Father of the universe (Philo, ibid.), and the first-born Son of God (Philo, *de agricult.* 1.1).

Thus, you see St. John speaks of Christ in such a manner, as both Jews and Gentiles might understand of whom he spoke, namely of a divine Person, a divine Subsistence. The Apostles, when they preached Christ to the Jews and Gentiles, used such words as were known to them and understood by them. They coined no new ones, nor did they put new constructions upon them unknown to the world before. They spoke in the plainest and most intelligible manner and made use of such words as Jews and Gentiles had used before, that both Jews and Gentiles might understand them.

When, therefore, St. John speaks of his Word, and in the same phrase and language gives the same account of him as the Jewish and Gentile divines did of theirs, he must be taken to mean the same thing, namely that the Word is a divine eternal Person. How else would anyone take him? For he who speaks or writes in common phrases must use those words according to the common meaning of those words and phrases. If he does not, he must be a most notorious juggler and hypocrite.

Thus, if St. John wrote sincerely what he thought of Christ, every man who reads him and understands his words must believe that that Christ is a divine Person, and that he is the Savior. That John was so understood by Amelius (3rd cent), a pagan philosopher (who understood the language and doctrine of the Gentile schools very well concerning the divine Word so often mentioned in their writings) appears; for he calls his eyes upon the text of St. John, and then does with all confidence affirm that this was that Word, who, according to Heraclitus (500 BC), existed from eternity, and made all things, and whom, by Jupiter, the Barbarian (meaning the Evangelist) places in the order and dignity of a Principal, declaring him to have been with God, and to be God, and that all things were made by him, and that in him all things that were had life and being (Euseb. *Prep. Gospel*).

And now having proved at large that this Memra, this Logos, this Word is a divine Person, is the Messiah, is the Son of God, the eternal God which is the great hinge upon which this whole Discourse turns; I proceed to assert that it is certain from Moses that God appeared to several of the Patriarchs, which must necessarily therefore be this Memra, the Word of God. And this is what the Christian Fathers assert, that Christ the Son of God made several appearances to the ancient Patriarchs, in the assumption of human bodies, which were momentary assumptions only, and figurative of the perfect and lasting union of the divine Nature of the Son of God with Humanity.[77]

---

[77] De Gols seems to cite Leo the Great here (Ep. 27. Ad Pulcher c.2). I think there is much reason to disagree that the body was either human (it was angelic) or temporary (it went back up to heaven, a real and permanent place where the Angel was worshiped as God in the heavenly throne-room; see Isaiah 6:1).

Our Saviour, telling the Jews that *they had not heard the Father's voice at any time, nor seen his shape or appearance* (John 5:37), is full proof that that divine Person who appeared and spoke to the patriarchs in a human voice or shape was not God the Father. Yet, it is as positively said that Moses, and Aaron, and the elders of the Jews, and several others saw God. It necessarily follows that the God who appeared to them was the Second Person, distinct from the Father, and yet the self-same God. And this is Jesus, whose name is called the Word of God (Rev 19:13).

CHAP. VIII.

CHRIST WORSHIPED BY THE PATRI- ARCHS FROM ADAM TO MOSES

I come now to the facts, and these I shall take leave to divide into three great epochs.

First, the age of the Patriarchs, from Adam to Moses. Second, the epoch of the Mosaic dispensation from Moses to Christ. Third, the great epoch of the Gospel from Christ to this day.

In all these periods of time Jesus Christ has been adored as God, and worshiped with the Father, and the Holy Spirit, as the one only true and supreme God.

First, The Age of the Patriarchs.

Eusebius asserts that all the Patriarchs were the Christians of the old world, who had the same faith, re- ligion, worship, and the same Name of Christians too. This he endeavors to prove from Psalm 105:15, *Touch not my anointed (tōn Christōn mou) my Christians*, or *my Christs* (Eus. *Prep. Gospel* 1.4.9). But more particularly,

Adam worshiped Christ as God.

It is generally agreed among Divines, that Adam in the state of perfection knew God in Trinity and

Unity.[78] Epiphanius (*Panario*) is most positive in this point. He says Adam was not an idolater, for he knew the Father God, and the Son, and the Holy Ghost; for he was a prophet, and knew that the Father had said to the Son, *Let US make Man*. The same Epiphanius carries that matter a great deal higher and says that Adam, even in the state of perfection, was a Christian, having the form of Christianity, for he was not circumcised; neither was he an idolater, but had the form of Christianity. And Jerome Zanchi (*de creat* 1.1.c.1§12) thinks it very injurious to Adam to believe that he had not as great favor shown him before the Fall as Abraham, Moses, and others had since the Fall. He thus asserts that Adam was sure of the beloved of God, because Jehovah the Son exhibited himself visibly to him, and talked with him, and made himself known to him as his God and Governor before he gave him the precepts of obedience, as he did to the Jews before he gave the Law to Moses. He tells us that several of the ancients (Justin, Irenaeus, Tertullian, and many more) were of that mind that it was Jehovah the Son who created Adam, placed him in Paradise, appeared visibly to him, discoursed with him, and whose voice he heard, and at which he trembled when he had transgressed.

---

[78] Johanni Markii, *Compendium Theol. Christianæ* (C. 1. § 16); Herman Witsius, *The Economy of the Covenants between God and Man: Comprehending a Complete Body of Divinity*, I.2.5.

If, therefore, Adam was so well acquainted with the Son of God before his fall and knew and feared him after he had fallen, there is no doubt but he very well understood the gracious promise of Genesis 3:15, namely that by the promised Seed the same God, Jehovah the Son, would restore him and his offspring from that misery they had brought upon themselves. Because Eve had been first in the transgression, he would restore them by the *Seed of the Woman.*

This promise was the first Gospel, the only Article of Faith that the Serpent's head by whom they fell should be bruised by the Seed of the Woman. It was a promise. It was the first promise. As a promise, it was made *in Christ, in whom all the promises are Yes and Amen* (2Co 1:20).

The Jews in their Targums acknowledge that the Seed of the woman is the Messiah. So we find it in the Jerusalem Targum: "And it shall be when the Children of the Woman shall study the Law, and perform the commandments, that they shall be ready to strike you (O Serpent) upon the Head, and kill you, but when the children of the woman shall forsake the commands of the Lord, and not perform the statutes, you shalt be ready to bite them upon the heels, and hurt them. But there shall be a remedy for the children of the woman. But for you, O Serpent, there shall be no remedy. But the time shall come that they shall from one to another apply remedies to their heels, at the end of the extremity of days, in the days of King Messiah."

In Jonathan's Targum, "And they will have a remedy for their heels in the days of the Messiah."

It is evident that mother Eve herself understood that that Seed of the woman was to be God; for being so forward as to think that the restoration from the fall was to be performed presently by her first-born, she cried out immediately upon the birth of her first child, *I have gotten that Man which is Jehovah the Lord*, or else, *I have gotten that man from the Lord, who was promised to be the Deliverer.*

Why our version reads it, *I have gotten a man from the Lord*, when the words will bear, and ought to bear the other construction,[79] I doubt not. For there is no doubt, as Dr. Lightfoot observes, but Eve had regard to the promise of a Saviour, and therefore said she had obtained that man the Jehovah (*ish et-yhwh*; *ton anthrōpon ton kurion*), that God, that Jehovah, which should become man.[80] The Chaldee paraphrase of Jonathan reads that verse this way, "And Adam knew Eve his wife, who exceedingly longed for that Angel (who was to restore them to happiness) and she conceived and bore Cain, and said, 'I have gotten that Man that

---

[79] He cites a work from the Reformer Paul Fagius (1504-49), *Commentary on Genesis 4*.
[80] John Lightfoot, *A Commentary on the New Testament from the Talmud and Hebraica, Matthew-1 Corinthians, Acts-1 Corinthians*, vol. 4 (Bellingham, WA: Logos Bible Software, 2010), 275.

is the Angel of Jehovah'" (TGen 4:1). And an ancient Belgic, "I have obtained that man of the Lord." And in the annotations has this paraphrase, that is, "Blessed be God, here I have the Lord, the Man, that Seed, who shall bruise the Head of Satan, or the Serpent, he shall perform it."[81]

This is certain however, that mother Eve made a very singular confession of the person of the Messiah, that she looked for him as the *Theanthropos*—God and man. She declares him a man when she calls him *ish*, a man; not Adam, but *virum*, to signify his excellency. For those words differ, Adam-man signifying the weakness of human nature, but *ish*-man signifying the excellency of human nature. She professes his divine nature when she calls him Jehovah. That those natures were to be united in one person, the Redeemer, when she joins these two *ish et-yhwh, the man that is the Lord*; which St. Paul expresses by *Theon ephanerōthē en sarki* (1Ti 3:16).[82]

It is very remarkable that Adam did not call his wife *Chava*, or Eve, the mother of all livings until after he had received the promise of the Messiah. Before this, he called her *Ishah*, Woman. But when God had assured him of a Saviour, a Deliverer, then he calls her Eve, or Life, for so the LXX rendered it, *kai ekalesen Adam to onoma tes gunaikos autou Zōē* (Gen 3:20). And

---

[81] He cites the *biblia Belgic*, 1581 at Delft, annot. In c. iv. 1 and older Belgicc versions of 1559 and 1562 read the same way.
[82] See Witsius, *Economy* 2.4.19.

why so? Why must she be called Life, who was in the Introducer of Death? The reason is because Adam knew that in the promised Seed, the "last Adam" (*eschatos Adam*) was included and signified; and that he should be "quickening Spirit" (*pneuma zōopoioun*), as St. Paul calls Christ (1Co 15:45), that he should introduce a better life; thus he is also called Life (John 1:4).[83]

Cain and Abel worshiped Christ as God.

That Cain and Abel believed that same gospel or promise of a Saviour cannot be doubted; for upon faith in the Seed of the woman, the man Jehovah (as their mother had explained it), they both offered their sacrifices to God.

The word sacrifice, though it has often been used for all the duties of divine worship, yet seems here to relate to that external form of worship which is called "expiation" (*hilasmos*), which they offered to God in all probability in order to obtain pardon for their parents transgression, and the release of that misery which their sin had brought upon them and their offspring.

And though we do not find when God was first pleased to institute these sacrificial rites, yet it is piously believed they were of his own appointment,[84]

---

[83] Lightfoot, ibid., and Witsius, ibid.
[84] Dr. Heylin *on the Creed*, p. 93.

because of his acceptance and confirmation, and because he afterwards instituted them by most positive precepts. And no doubt but these very first sacrifices, as they were offered up to God with a view to the promised Seed, the Man-Jehovah, were figures of that one only real and propitiatory sacrifice of Christ, who, through the eternal Spirit, was to offer up himself without spot to God for the redemption of the world (Heb 9:14). For these sacrificial rites had no propitiatory power in them by themselves, of their own nature, but only by virtue of the divine institution, by the ordinance of Almighty God, and by the relation they had to the Messiah the Saviour. Such is should not be doubted were the sacrifices of Cain and Abel, and therefore as such offered to the Son of God as believing in him as the promised Seed—the Man-Jehovah.

Though it may be said that Cain's offering seemed rather to be a "Sacrifice of Thanksgiving" (*eucharistia*), which he offered to God as a quit-rent,[85] in testimony that he held his estate from him as the supreme Landlord, and that Abel's seemed only expiatory; I shall only answer that we know so little of that

---

[85] Effectively but not formally a tax or land tax imposed on freehold or leased land by a higher landowning authority, usually a government or its assigns. Under feudal law, the payment of quit rent freed the tenant of a holding from the obligation to perform such other services as were obligatory under feudal tenure or freed the occupier of the land from the burden of having others use their own distinct rights that affected the land.

matter that all we can say is but conjecture. But it is plain that Cain's offering was not accepted, and this was not from any mistake in the object of his worship, nor in the subject of his oblation, but through the default of his own heart; and St. Paul I think tells us that his faith was not so strong as Abel's (Heb 11:4). *"By faith Abel offered to God a more excellent sacrifice than Cain,"* so that Cain's crime was unbelief. Of what? Of the promised Seed of the Man-Jehovah, the Redeemer, of Christ, as the Apostle there recommends from the happy examples of the elders. And if St. Paul is a good expositor of the Faith of the elders, as he undoubtedly is, then according to him they believed in, and offered to Jesus Christ, and of faith in him: and if we continue in that faith, it will produce the same happy effects in us as it did in the worthies mentioned in the 11th Chapter, who believed in Christ Jesus, and by that faith received the testimony that they pleased God. That they all believed in Christ, is sure from that instance of Moses, of whom it is said expressly that he believed in Christ (vs. 26). *"He considered the reproach of Christ greater wealth than the treasures of Egypt, for he was looking to the reward."*

That they both believed a Savior to come seems to be plain from Gen 4:7. *"If you do well, will you not be accepted? And if you do not do well, sin is crouching at the door."* You must observe that the original word "sin" can also signify an expiation for sin, so that the verse will bear this reading: "*If you do not do well, then not only the sin itself, not only the guilt and punishment, but also the expiation for sin, the sacrifice of propitiation, lies ready at the door: for if you do well, you may be sure of being rewarded, but if you do otherwise you ought not to despair of being for-given, nor be terribly dejected, because the mercy of God is greater than your sin; and for your countenance to fall is not right, seeing that the atonement is ready by faith as the Lamb of God is represented in the sacrifice of Abel, which is a most acceptable sin-offering.*" For the design of this text is evidently the silencing and quieting of the spirit criminally agitated by violent commotions.[86]

The paraphrase of Onkelos proves what we have just said. "*If you will do well, shall you not be pardoned? But if you will not do well, shall not your sin be reserved against the Day of Judgment, when it shall be revenged upon you, if you will not be converted? Whereas if you will be converted, it shall be forgiven you.*" In a word, that the only true God and the promised Seed was the object of religious worship is certain. For idolatry was not established until long after, according to the Jews, who expound the 26th verse of this chapter, "*Then men began to call on the Name of the Lord,*" or, as our margin has it, to call themselves by the Name of the Lord, that is, in

---

[86] De Gols cites Samuel Parker (1681-1730), *Bibliotheca Biblica: Being A Commentary Upon All the Books of the Old and New Testament Gathered Out of the Genuine Writings of the Fathers and Ecclesiastical Historians, and Acts of Councils, Down to the year of our Lord 451* (Oxford: William and John Innys, 1720). The citations in what follows are from Volume 1: Genesis (Part I). See Gen 4:7, p. 160.

distinction from idolatry, which then received its first establishment, and which was, according to Mr. Perkins, *Anno Mundi* 235, more than 200 years after.

Enoch worshiped Christ as God.

That Enoch knew and worshiped Christ as God, is not only probable, as being a descendent from ancestors noted for being truly religious, but is very certain from Gen 5:24 where he has this grand character given him, "*and Enoch walked with God;*" that is, as the Targum of Jonathan explains that verse, "Enoch worshiped in truth before the Lord, and behold he is not numbered among the generations of the earth, for he was taken away from it, and ascended into heaven by the Word before the Lord." And the Jerusalem Targum says, "Enoch worshiped before the Lord in the Truth, and thus he was not! because he was translated by the Word of the Presence of the Lord."

An ancient Targumist (Pseudo-Jonathan) further says, "Enoch, ascended into Heaven by the Word of the Lord, and his Name is called Metatron, the great scribe." This is to say that he, being translated from the earth, by the power of the eternal Word and Son of God, has thereupon become a ministering spirit to the spirits of the prophets, and a great angelical prince under him in that order. According to this, the name of the angel who took him up at the command of the

Lord should be Metatron, which is the Name commonly given by the learned Jews to the Angel of the Shekinah itself, when written with a yod.[87]

From these expositions of the Jews we may be very sure that Enoch not only believed in the promised Seed, the Man Jehovah, but worshiped him as Jehovah. And if their authority is not sufficient, I am very sure St. Paul's is, who numbers him among those heroes who were famous for their faith in Christ (Heb 11:5), and St. Jude the Apostle mentions this very man as a prophet of Christ, who spoke of Christ, and foretold his Coming to Judgment, *"Behold, the Lord comes with ten thousands of his holy ones, to execute judgment"* (Jude 1:14-15); which can pertain to no one but Christ, as that expression "the Lord comes," is frequently used concerning Christ, as we see in 1Th 4:15, 16 and elsewhere. Concerning that prophecy, I shall only observe that Drusius[88] says that it is to this day extant among the Ethiopians in the Abyssine language; but whether different from that which St. Augustine (*City of God* 15.23) has long since pronounced not genuine, I cannot say.[89]

---

[87] *Biblioth. Biblica*, Occasion. Annot. 11. P. 187.

[88] Johannes Drusius (1550-1616). Dutch scholar, Orientalist, Christian Hebraist and exegete. While De Gols does not cite a book, it is probable it comes from *Henoch; sive, De Patriarcha Henoch* (1612).

[89] While Drusius and others such as Nicolas-Claude Fabri de Peiresc (1580-1637) were speculating about the existence of what we now call 1 Enoch, it was not until 1773, 50 years after De Gols writes *A Vindication*, when James Bruce brought three Ethiopian copies of the book back to England, that it was confirmed that Jude was in fact

I shall only observe that St. Paul, when he speaks of Enoch, says that he had this testimony that he pleased God; wherein he followed not the original Hebrew, but the LXX translation, which has rendered, "*And Enoch walked with God,* by "Enoch pleased God" (*euērestēsen de Enoch tō Theō*); and the Syriac in the same manner, "he pleased God," which indeed is tantamount, because he could not please God without walking with God, and he could not walk with God without pleasing him. The LXX has rendered the same expression concerning Noah in the same words (Gen 6:9), so though the original has not the word of pleasing God, yet the sense is the same, the one being the exposition of the other, namely, that to walk with God is to please God.

Noah worshiped Christ as God.

That Noah worshiped God and lived in a pious obedience to the will of God is certain from that extraordinary character given him (Gen 6:9). "*Noah was a just man, and perfect in his generations, and Noah walked with God;*" which last is the same expression used of Enoch (Gen 5:24) and is explained in Gen 7:1, "*I have seen that you are righteous before me in this generation.*" That he knew and worshiped the Son of God is as

---

quoting from 1 Enoch 1:9. As the writing of 1 Enoch clearly dates to the time before the NT and the Epistle of Jude was written, De Gols' argument is strengthened that Enoch in fact spoke of the Messiah.

plain, because the God that spoke to Noah is called the Lord, the Jehovah (7:1), that Person of the sacred Trinity by whom all revelations were made and communications held with mankind. He is by the Targums called the "*Word of the Lord.*" This is confirmed by St. Paul, who numbers this great man among the ancient heroes, who are recorded for their faith in Christ the Son of God (Heb 11:7), and is further confirmed in that the very flood was an act of judgment executed by the Son of God, because all judgment is given to the Son.[90] St. Peter also tells us expressly that Christ preached repentance to the world in the days of Noah, while the Ark was preparing (1Pe 3:19-20; 2Pe 2:5), and that Noah was his servant and minister who is therefore, by St. Peter, called the preacher of righteousness. And when it is said, "*The Lord shut Noah in the Ark*" (Gen 7:16), this was the act and deed of the Son of God.[91] And at his delivery he built an altar to the LORD, to the Word of the LORD, in thanksgiving for his redemption, the figure and pledge of a far greater (1Pe 3:20).

The ancient Jews have a tradition that in the ark there was a "place of prayer," where there was an appearance of the Glory of the LORD, the divine Shekinah, which is the Son of God, as I shall now unfold for you. Before this Glory, Noah daily offered up

---

[90] Hilary, Psalm 63, col. 160.
[91] Tertullian, *Against Praxeas* 16.

prayers and intercessions. And the said tradition further adds that this chapel was at or about the center of the Ark, and that the body of Adam, enclosed in a shrine which had been preserved and handed down from father to son, was placed in this very chapel in the Ark at the very place where the Glory of God appeared. Every morning at day-break, as uncovered by the Zohar, or heavenly Light that was in the Ark,[92] Noah stood up towards the body of Adam and before the Lord, and the Shekinah appeared over it, and he and his sons made this prayer:

> O Lord, you are excellent in your truth and there is nothing great in comparison to you. Look upon us with the eye of mercy and compassion. Deliver us from this deluge of waters and set our feet in a larger room. By the sorrows of Adam, your first-made man; by the blood of Abel, your holy one; by the righteousness of Seth, in whom you are well pleased, number us not among those who have transgressed your statutes. But take us into your merciful care, for you are our Deliverer and to you is the praise for all the works of your hands forevermore.

And then all the sons of Noah cried, "Amen, Lord."[93]

---

[92] *Biblioth. Bibl.* Occasion. Annot. 11. P. 202 in Gen.
[93] Mr. John Gregory's Notes on Heb 12:23.

Whatever may be thought of this prayer, the truth of the tradition seems liable to no objection, namely,

> That the sanctuary of God was within the Ark, and that Noah officiated as High-Priest from inside, making atonement by the blood of Christ, prefigured by that of Abel; and at the same time representing the miserable state of fallen man in Adam, and the happy deliverance out of it by the righteousness of that true Seth, or substitute, in whom God is well-pleased.

And so the Ark is to be considered as a consecrated place of worship of which the center was the body of the first Adam, overshadowed by the Glory of the body of the Second Adam. Thus, from the sacredness of the Ark and the appearance there of the Shekinah,[94] and the manner of Noah's worshiping, the Ark was anciently called *Haical*, the temple, or the church of God.

But further, that Noah worshiped the Son of God, is plain from the covenant of God with Noah after the Flood. For when God gave him a visible token of that covenant, not to destroy the world again by water, it is expressed, "*The covenant which I make between me and you … between me and the earth*" (Gen 11:12-13). Now the Targums will tell us who the

---

[94] *Biblioth. Biblic.* Annot. on Gen 14, p. 241.

Person covenanting with Noah and the earth was, for they all unanimously interpret "between my Word and you," and "between my Word and the earth;" as if the divine Logos, or Christ, was made a party in the covenant. This is repeated no less than four times in vv. 15-16 from which it is eminently manifest that Noah worshiped Christ as God.

Melchizedek worshiped Christ as God.

That Melchizedek worshiped Christ as God, I think is beyond all doubt; for he was both a type of Christ and priest to Christ the Son of God. In Genesis 14:18 he is called "the priest of the Most High God," and in vs. 19 in his benediction he invokes the Most High God, possessor of heaven and earth. In this he invokes the holy Trinity, the great God essentially taken, and there is no doubt but Melchizedek knew God as such. But it is very likely that this man had received some peculiar revelation whereby he was appointed a priest to the Most High God, and that must be the Son, by whom all revelations were made. This is doubtless the reason. Hilary says this Most High God is our Lord Jesus Christ,"[95] Epiphanius says, the first person we find officiating in the priesthood of uncircumcision was Abel, the second was Noah, and

---

[95] Hilary, *On the Trinity* 12.4.

the third was Melchizedek,[96] and as a priest, St. Paul largely speaks of him as the type of Christ (Heb 7:1ff). It would be very strange for him to be a type of Christ and at the same time a priest of a god different from Christ, and that the Most High God is the title of Christ, we have seen before. Though we know but little of this great man, and what is said of him beside what we find in the Scriptures, is conjecture only. We find from what is said of him that the Christian Fathers have believed him to have known and worshiped Christ as his priest,[97] and declared Christ to the Gentiles. For so Epiphanius,[98] and Gregory Nazianzen. "This Melchizedek was king, as well as priest, among the Gentiles; in which several capacities he was the type and representative of Christ, that great archetypal King and Priest, who offered himself a sacrifice for all mankind."[99]

I am not ignorant that several of the ancients[100] and moderns[101] are of opinion that this Melchizedek was not a man, but the Lord Jesus Christ himself, who appeared to Abraham in the way, and blessed him as the priest of the Most High God, the great Messenger (Angel) of Peace; and that thereupon Abraham offered to him tithes; and that both were figures, one of

---

[96] Epiphanius, *Against Melchizedekians* 55.3.1.
[97] Augustine, *City of God* 17.5.5.
[98] Epiphanius, *Against Melchizedekians* 55.3.1.
[99] Gregory Nazianzen, *Oration* 36.
[100] Ravanel. Bibliothec. Ver. Zelchiz. Suiceri Thesaur. Ver. Melchiz.
[101] Cunaei Rep. Hebr. 1.2.c.3. See Spanheim tom. 2. P. 189. Fol.

Christ's future office, the other of the Churches future submission and obedience; and that this priest offered bread and wine, a type of the Eucharist, to repast (a meal) the whole Christian Church,[102] as he did Abraham's army here. But this is beside my present purpose.

Abraham worshiped Christ as God.

I come now to that great instance of faith and piety, the father of the faithful, Abraham, of whom St. Paul gives a very large account both of his heroic faith and heroic obedience—his faith in Christ and his obedience to Christ (Heb 11:8-19).

That Abraham both knew and worshiped the Son of God, we shall find as clear as the day from the following particulars.

In Genesis 12:1 and 7 we find that the Lord appeared to Abram. This appearance language is the first that we read of where God is said to have explicitly made himself visible to any man, for it never unambiguously says he conversed visibly with Adam, Abel, Noah, or any other. That this Lord was Christ is not only asserted by the Christian writers,[103] but by the Jews themselves, who own that all the appearances of God were made by the (*mmr'*) Memra, the Word of the LORD, who is the Logos, the Son of God.

---

[102] *Biblioth. Bib.* In Gen 14:18. P. 348.
[103] Tertullian, *Against Marcion*; *Against Praxeas*. Eusebius, *Demonstration of the Gospel*, and many others.

Thus, we find that, "*After these things the word of the LORD came to Abram in a vision: 'Fear not, Abram, I am your shield; your reward shall be very great'*" (Gen 15:1).[104] This is the first time that this expression of the Word of the Lord is found in Scripture; and if one text may explain another, as is agreed by all men, then it appears from John 1:1 that this Word of the Lord was Christ. And this is further explained in vs. 6 where it is said, "*He believed in the Lord, and it was counted to him as righteousness.*" What did he believe? Was his faith only concerning the number of his offspring or concerning the Messiah, "*That in your all the families of the earth shall be blessed*" (Gen 11:3)? If St. Paul understood it right, as he most certainly did, he tells us that this faith principally related to Christ. He believed indeed that God was able to make his offspring as numerous as the stars in the heavens (Rom 4:19), but he principally believed the promise of God, that the Savior, the Messiah, who is Christ, should be of his Seed (Gal 3:16) and was justified by his faith in the Savior.[105]

This is the second degree of the revelation of Christ. Thus far, the faithful only had the promise of the Seed of the woman to rely upon, but of whom that

---

[104] De Gols inexplicably deletes the vital words, "in a vision," which is found in the KJV and all older English translations as well as the Hebrew and Greek. This surely would have bolstered his point even further, given that the Word is here expressly visible to the eye.

[105] Irenaeus, *Against Heresies.*

Seed was to come, or by what family, was yet a secret. But now God revealed to Abraham that it should be in his seed, and St. Paul says directly that this Seed was Christ (Gal 3:16).

To confirm that promise, God gave him the sacrament of circumcision, and promised to be his God and protector in this life and his Savior in the life to come. For that sacrament was the seal of the covenant of God in Christ, and of Abraham's faith in Christ, as the Redeemer, for the gospel was preached to Abraham (Gal 3:8, 16-17) and the covenant was confirmed to Abraham in Christ (17).

Again, we find that Abraham worshiped the Son of God as God, and called him Lord and Judge of all the earth, in his intercession for Sodom (Gen 18:25).

From the account given us in that chapter, it is plain that the Lord appeared to Abraham, and that Abraham prayed to him and worshiped him. But how? With a civil worship? No, with a religious adoration, for he worshiped him as God, and as Lord of the whole earth. "For in this narration he is called God and Lord, which is a style," says Eusebius,[106] "too high for any angelical power, and therefore was the Logos, the Son of God, whom he adored." And Justin Martyr[107] proves largely against the Jews that the person who here appeared to Abraham was God the Son. And

---

[106] Eusebius, *Demonstration of the Gospel* 1.5.c.9.
[107] Justin, *Dialogue with Trypho.*

the Fathers of the Council of Antioch[108] in their excellent Epistle against Paul of Samosata, express themselves so fully and strongly, and yet so comprehensively upon this and the corresponding passages of the patriarchal history, that their argumentation deserves to appear in all its force.

> This Son of God, personally distinct from the Father, appeared to Abraham at the Oak of Mamre; he was that one of the three in human shape, with whom the Patriarch discoursed, *as with the universal Lord and Judge (hōs Kyriō kai kritē)*. He was the Lord that rained fire and brimstone upon Sodom and Gomorrah from the Lord out of Heaven; he was his holy Father's agent in his communications with the Patriarchs, and is the same Person under the several denominations of the Angel, of the divine counsel, of the Lord, and of God. Now certainly it must argue rank impiety and irreligion, to think that Moses would have called any angelic power "the God of the universe," of the whole creation; and yet he that is this LORD and God, is both the Son and the Angel, or Administrator of the Father.

If we compare this account of Moses with John 8:56 it will appear from Christ's own words that Abraham both saw him and worshiped him too.

---

[108] De Gols refers to the Letter of Six Bishops in 268 AD. We have translated the entire letter in our book on the Angel of the LORD.

That verse reads, "*Your father Abraham rejoiced to see my day. He saw it and was glad.*" Now the seeing of Christ's day must necessarily signify his real, actual, and proper sight of Christ himself; and so the Jews understood it, "*You are not yet fifty years old, and you have seen Abraham?*" (57) who has been dead many ages. And that they did understand Christ right is evident, because otherwise Christ would have corrected them, had they mistook or misapprehended him. But Christ allows their sense, and approves of their interpretation, and answers them in the same sense they put it to him by saying, "*Truly, truly, I say to you, before Abraham was, I am*" (John 8:58), thereby signifying his eternal existence. For I AM is one of the names of God, of his eternity, "*from everlasting to everlasting you are God*" (Ps 90:2). And so the text may be paraphrased, "It was no such difficult matter for Abraham to see my day, since I have a fixed, an eternal existence, and was in being before Abraham was born." And upon this foundation that the Council at Sirmium (351 A.D.), against Photinus, annexed this anathema to the creed,[109] "If any one shall affirm that it was not the Son which appeared to Abraham, but the ineffable Father, let him be accursed."

Further, we find that Abraham worshiped the Lord Christ as God and obeyed him as such in the sacrifice of his son Isaac.

---

[109] Hilary, de Syn. col. 1176.

We find when God tempted or tried Abraham's faith and obedience, he used the name of Elohim, which according to the Jewish doctors is the name of Judgment; but afterwards, when the sacrifice was accepted, the oblation was released by the Angel of the LORD (Gen 22:11-12). *"For the Angel of the LORD said, 'Do not lay your hand on the boy or do anything to him.'"* From this text St. Augustine proves that this Angel was no creature, but God himself, the Son of God that accepted the intention and released the offering, for that God now appeared by the Name of Jehovah, which is the Name of Mercy, or of God covenanted with man; for which end the Angel or Messenger of the covenant is sent to preside over this great transaction (and to see it performed, and by substitution to redeem the sacrifice) who is called the Angel of the Lord.[110]

And that this Angel of the LORD was the Son of God is not only the exposition of the Christians,[111] but must necessarily be, because we find that Angel expressing himself in these words, *"'By myself I have sworn,' says the LORD"* (Gen 22:16), which none can say but God. Or, as the Targums[112] read it, "By my Word have I sworn," which is therefore necessarily

---

[110] Augustine, *Questions on Genesis* 59.
[111] St. Cyprian, Against the Jews 1.ii. § 5; Letter of the Six; Cyril of Alexandria, *cont. Julian* 1.9. p. 293. Who renders it, "By myself have I sworn," i.e. "By my eternal Son, of one Essence with myself."
[112] Onkelos and Jonathan.

God. That same Angel (vs. 17-18) expresses his benediction to Abraham in his posterity, and to all nations
of the earth by his posterity, because of Abraham's
obedience to his voice, in terms so lofty, and assuming
a power which none but the eternal God enjoys.

I shall only add that we find Abraham built an altar to the LORD, and that the LORD was an Angel,
which shows that the Angel was the eternal God; for
had Abraham not known him as such, he would never
have built an altar to him, for that was the highest act
of the most solemn adoration. Had this Angel not
been God, he would no more have permitted that
worship than the Angel which forbade Manoah (Jdg
13:16)[113] or the other which hindered St. John (Rev
22:9). I cannot refrain from saying that Abraham's
faith in Christ was so singularly great that he is not
only called the father of the faithful (Rom 4:11)
whose faith and obedience is set before all the world
for imitation, but that even heaven itself, the purchase
of the blood of Christ, is called by the name of Abraham's Bosom (Luke 16:22), that Harbor of Rest and
Place of Honor which all the saints of God shall enjoy
who follow the faith and imitate the obedience of
faithful Abraham.

---

[113] It is not certain that De Gols' interpretation of this verse with
Manoah says that the Angel did not permit the worship of him. It could
easily be interpreted that the Angel was telling Manoah that he is the
LORD and that it is to the LORD, that is him rather than a mere creature, that he should offer his offering. This is actually De Gols' point
later on.

It is beside my present purpose to explain the reason of that expression; but we may be very sure that the Lord Jesus would never have called the state of rest "Abraham's Bosom," had not Abraham believed in him and obeyed him as the God and Savior of the World.

I have purposely omitted the opinion that the three Persons of the Holy Trinity, Father, Son, and Holy Ghost, appeared to Abraham at Mamre, and were known by him as such, and yet confronted by him in the singular number, and adored in the unity of the divinity by him; because though many of the ancients, and some moderns are of that opinion, it seems not to be very well grounded, but liable to some exceptions, notwithstanding it has been largely defended by a late learned writer.[114]

Further, I have omitted the opinion of Cunæus,[115] that Christ appeared to Abraham in the very self-same form, features, and countenance as he afterwards had when in the flesh; and that this should be approved by John 8:56 because it is singular and stands in need of confirmation.

Hagar worshiped Christ as God.

That Hagar was instructed in the true religion, in the knowledge of the Triunal God, and the covenant of

---

[114] Witsius, *Economy of the Divine Covenants* 4.3.4.
[115] Petrus Cunæus (Peter van der Kun, 1586-1638). Dutch Christian Rabbinical scholar at the University of Leyden. The work is *The Hebrew Republic* (Amsterdam, 1682), 1.3. c. 3. P. 414.

grace, and the expectation of a Savior, there is no room to doubt, being of Abraham's family; especially if we consider what God himself says of Abraham. *"For I have chosen him, that he may command his children and his household after him to keep the way of the LORD"* (Gen 18:19).

I have nothing to do at present with her perhaps too easy readiness to comply with her mistress's desire to receive her master's embraces. Though, I freely own, I do not understand that surrogation whereby several of the Christian Fathers have excused the ancient Patriarchs.[116] My business is Hagar's religion, and I may venture to say that she knew, believed, and adored the Son of God.

Genesis 16:7. We find that the Angel of the LORD appeared to Hagar. Who that Angel was we find in vs. 10. He is the one who blessed in his own name and by his own authority. Then, in vs. 13, *"She called the name of the LORD who spoke to her, 'You God see me."*[117] Thus, it is certain that the Angel who spoke to her was God.

The Targumists say that Hagar prayed in the name of the LORD, saying, *"You are a God seeing all things, because she said, 'I have begun to see since he appeared to me;' therefore she called the well, The Well Over Which Appeared the Angel of Life."*

---

[116] *Biblioth. Bib.* In Gen Occas. Annot. 33. Tecnopoeia, p. 649.
[117] This is my modern rendition of the KJV. Most translations say something like, "You are a God of seeing." The KJV makes De Gols' point a little more strongly.

The Jews will have it that God was inclined in like manner to manifest himself to Sarah, as to a prophetess, by virtue of the relation she bore to Abraham; and that for his sake, this Angel was also sent to Hagar. The Jerusalem paraphrast describes this fully, "And Hagar gave thanks and prayed in the name of the Word of the LORD, who had appeared to her, saying, 'Blessed be you, O God, who are the enlivener of all worlds, in that you have had regard to my affliction, for behold now to me also has God appeared after the same manner he was pleased to manifest himself to Sarah my lady." But Jonathan supposes that the very Shekinah, the Person of the Son of God, did appear to her; wherefore according to him, she gave thanks before the LORD whose Word has spoken to her, and spoke, "You are he who lives and makes alive, who beholds and are not beheld; for behold, here was the Glory of the Shekinah of the LORD revealed."

Lot worshiped Christ as God.

That Lot knew and worshiped Christ as God, I think is plain from the history of his deliverance from the judgment of Sodom.

For although we find that two angels came to him (Gen 19:1), which are expressly so called to let us know their natures, yet is seems from vs. 19 that the LORD, the Memra, the Logos, the Word had come to them. For there we find Lot praying to him. He confesses himself his servant and magnifies his mercy for sparing his life, which not the angel but God himself had spared. In vs. 21 the Angel says, "*I have accepted you,*" which no angel could say nor would have the power to do. And it is plain from vs. 24 that the LORD executed the judgment "*from the LORD out of heaven.*" This proves that we have one LORD in Person distinct from the other LORD. Justin Martyr, St. Cyprian,[118] and others of the ancients assert that the LORD who executed this vengeance was God the Son, for all judgment was given to him by the Father (John 5:22).

Isaac worshiped Christ as God.

That Isaac worshiped Christ the Son of God as God is not only probable because he worshiped the God of his father Abraham, but it further appears from Genesis 26:2. Where "*The LORD appeared to Isaac*" and said, "*I will be with you,*" the Targums have rendered it, "My Word shall be with you, and be your defense."

This was the first time that God appeared to Isaac. That it was the Shekinah, the visible appearance of the Son of God, is plain from vv. 24-25 where we find that the LORD appeared to him a second time, and that Isaac built an altar there and called upon the

---

[118] Justin Martyr, *Dialogue* 127; Cyprian, *Against the Jews* 3.33. See also Eusebius, *Ecclesiastical History* 1.2.9; Cyril of Alexandria, *Comments on 1Jn 1:2*; Tertullian, *Against Praxeas* 13; and many others.

Name of the Lord, or according to the Targums, he called upon the Word of the LORD. There, Isaac was installed in all the privileges of his father Abraham, in the special rights of the *segullah* (possession) and <u>Shekinah</u> (glory). And it is remarkable that this manifestation of God to Isaac was made in the same place which had been so solemnly dedicated to the Name of the LORD, the Everlasting God (Gen 31:33). When he blessed his son Jacob, he called upon God by the Name of God Almighty (28:3), El Shaddai, the All-Sufficient; which is the same name (17:1) in which the covenant of grace was erected, and therefore has relation to the Son. Thus, the LXX has emphatically rendered it the God in covenant with me (*ha Theos mou*).

Jacob worshiped Christ as God.

That Jacob worshiped the Lord Christ appears from Genesis 28:12ff. where the ladder, the scale of providence, is described. In vs. 13 it said that the LORD stood above it, and said, "*I am the LORD God.*"

I purpose not to talk tediously at length upon this vision, but shall only observe that the Targums interpret this by the Glory of the LORD, which is none other than Christ, the Glory and Image of the invisible Father, or the Shekinah of the divine Word and Wisdom with an angelical retinue. "Neither may this unfitly be said to be a prefiguration of the deity uniting with the human nature; for this is still the same Angel, and God, and LORD, even the Lord Jesus Christ, whom Abraham beheld with a human shape—who stood above the mystic ladder, and with whom Jacob wrestled.[119] That this ladder was a symbol of Christ, Christ himself gave Nathanael to understand (John 1:51).

Further, we find that when God told Jacob to return to Bethel (Gen 31), that the Angel said, "*I am the God of Bethel*" (vs. 13). Novatius has these words, "If no Angel could be so presumptuous as to call himself God and to mention a vow made to him, then it is plain that this is Christ the Son of God, the great Angel."[120] And the ancient rabbis believed that the man who wrestled with Jacob was the Christ (Messiah), the Son of God.[121] And indeed, the several parts of the history compared together demonstrate that the Person who here appeared to and encountered Jacob was the only begotten Son of God, God of God, very God of God.[122] And the creed of the Sirmian Council (351 AD), against Photinus, has this anathema added to it, "If any one shall affirm that it was the ineffable Father, or part or portion of him, and not the Son, that wrestled as a man with Jacob, let him be Anathema.[123] And

---

[119] Justin Martyr, *Dialogue* 58 in *Bibliotheca Biblica* on Gen 28:12 (p. 598).
[120] Novatian, *On The Trinity* 19.
[121] Ainsworth *in loc.* Gen 28.
[122] Theodoret, Q. in Genesis 93.
[123] Hilary, *On the Synod.* Col. 1176.

Eusebius delivers himself very exactly on this place in these words,

> Jacob did not see God the Father, the God over all, for he never exhibits himself visibly. He never appears in one and another place or form. He never joins himself to a human body, or shape, being supreme in being above all being. It was therefore another whom he saw. But if one now conceives that this "other" was a created angel, or any of those divine spirits in heaven who convey God's revelations to our senses, he is manifestly mistaken; for the Scripture expressly ascribes to him the style of "Lord" and "God;" even giving him that most sacred and peculiar designation of the four Letters [YHWH] which among the Jews denominate God himself.[124]

To put this matter beyond all doubt, the Holy Ghost has himself explained it by his prophet Hosea. *"In the womb he took his brother by the heel, and in his manhood he strove with God. He strove with the angel and prevailed; he wept and sought his favor. He met God at Bethel, and there God spoke with us—the LORD, the God of hosts, the LORD is his memorial Name"* (Hos 12:3-5).

Further, we find that God charged Jacob to go to Bethel (Gen 35:1) and there to erect an altar to the

---

[124] Eusebius, *Demonstration of the Gospel* 1.5.c.11.

God who appeared to him when he fled from his brother thirty years earlier.

This place is remarkable, and the ancients took notice of it. Hilary disputes with irresistible force against the Arians, "Here, says he, God speaks, and he of whom he speaks is God; the divine character is here equally ascribed to both in the community of the Name, and the subsistencies of both are as clearly distinguished."[125] Further, Jacob speaks of *"God who fed me"* and *"the Angel who redeemed me,"* as if they were one (Gen 48:15-16). It would be the greatest violence to grammatical construction and common sense to make the Angel in this verse one person and God in the former another; both being one and the same, in the nominative case to the verb bless. Nor can the God here, who is also called by the Name of Angel, be God the Father. He must be Christ, for Christ may truly be called both God and God's Angel or Agent.

Lastly, we find Jacob crying out, *"I have waited for your salvation, O LORD"* (Gen 49:18). In the Hebrew *Yeshuah* ("Salvation") expresses the very name of this desired Savior. When we find that Jacob erected altars to that God, that Angel, we must conclude that this Angel was the very eternal God. And this is confirmed by the Targum of Jerusalem, which introduces Jacob speaking to the twelve tribes in these words,

---

[125] Hilary, *On the Trinity* 1.4. § 30.

Do you worship the idols that Terah the Father of Abraham worshiped? Or do you worship the idols that Laban the brother of my mother worshiped? Or do you worship the God of Jacob? The twelve tribes answered together, with a perfect heart, and said, 'Hear now, O Israel our Father, the Lord our God is One God: Jacob answered and said, 'Let his great Name be blessed forever." (TDt 6:4)

Joseph worshiped Christ as God.

That Joseph knew and worshiped the God of his fathers is most certain; and that he worshiped the Son of God, we are assured by the authority of St. Paul, who numbers him among the heroes who were famous for their faith in, and reliance on, Jesus Christ the Son of God (Heb 11:22). He lived in the fear of God and his Savior (Gen 39:9), for it is said, *"The LORD was with him"* (21), which the Chaldee paraphrast renders, "The Word of the LORD was with him." That he died in the faith of Christ, or the Messiah, St. Paul tells us, *"By faith Joseph, at the end of his life, made mention of the exodus of the Israelites and gave directions concerning his bones"* (Heb 11:22). By this he testified his entire reliance on the promises of God made to his fore-fathers, and his belief of a resurrection from the dead, and the true rest in the Land of Promise above, typified by that here below.

CHAP. IX.

CHRIST WORSHIPED AS THE SUPREME GOD UNDER THE MOSAIC DISPENSATION

I come now to the second great epoch,

the Mosaic dispensation from Moses to Christ.

Moses worshiped Christ as God.

I come now to the great prophet Moses and declare that he knew and adored the Son of God, Jesus Christ as God and as the Savior of the world.

That Moses wrote of Christ is expressly declared by Christ himself, both before his death (John 5:46) and after his resurrection (Luke 24:27). That Moses was a faithful servant of Christ, St. Paul tells us (Heb 3:5). And that he believed in Christ, the same Apostle assures us (Heb 11:26). That he was a friend of God, we find in Exodus 33:11, and the greatest of the prophets; for he told the Jews even then, that God would raise them up a Prophet from among their brothers like him (Dt 18:18). And that this Prophet was Christ, we are assured by no less authority than that of St. John (John 1:45), St. Peter (Acts 3:22), and St. Stephen (Acts 7:37).

That the Son of God, as the God of the covenant, appeared to Moses, as he had done to the Patriarchs before, is beyond all contradiction; and that Moses worshiped him as the true and eternal God, will appear as evident, if we consult the history recorded in Exodus. Concerning this history, I shall make this observation only, that the account of the Exodus of Israel, and God's receiving them for his peculium,[126] and giving them the Law, is a most important history. For it regards that article of the divinity of the Logos or Word, the great Actor in this sacred transaction, against which the powers of hell have always exerted their utmost arts and violence and shown their fiercest rage and malice.

For here, the Angel of the LORD is not called the Angel of Elohim, as in Exodus 14:19, but the Angel of Jehovah (LORD), pointing completely to the gracious dispensation of that time. The Hebrew may be rendered not "the Angel of the LORD," but "the Angel, the LORD," or "the Jehovah," where the Angel of the LORD may reasonably be thought to be the Logos or Word. That is, the Lord the Messiah revealing himself to Moses as the Savior of his people Israel at that time, in the same way that he was pleased afterwards in the days of his flesh, namely at his transfiguration, to reveal

---

[126] This interesting word is well chosen and there are no direct synonyms for it in English. It refers to property that a father or master allowed his child or slave to hold as his own. In other words, by definition, the word implies that the Son has received Israel as his own in that it was given to him by the Father. Therefore, in this sentence, "God's receiving them" has to mean "Christ."

himself to this same Moses as the Savior of the world (Matt 17:3).

But let us consider the Person that is the prime Actor and the Legislator in this great affair.

This we find in Exodus 3:2, where the Person is called the Angel of the LORD, which is God the Son. For at the 4th verse he is called God, and he is called Angel, because he is the Angel of the great council, the mighty God, even Jesus Christ.[127] The Targums read it the Word of the LORD. At the 6th verse, this Angel styles himself, "*The God of Abraham, the God of Isaac, and the God of Jacob,*" and there it is also said that, "*Moses hid his face because he was afraid to look upon God.*" In vs. 14 he says his name is I AM THAT I AM. All of this demonstrates clearly that this Angel was God, truly and properly God, and yet not the Father, because the Father can in no sense be denominated as an Angel.[128] This was therefore God the Son, for no man has seen the Father and lived.[129]

And God the Son calls himself the God of Abraham, Isaac, and Jacob to let Moses know that he was the very God whom those great Patriarchs worshiped, the God who made the covenant with them, and the God who promised to be the deliverer of Israel. And that the name, *I am that I am,* is the proper name of Christ, and given to Christ, I have not only showed before, but is

---

[127] Justin Martyr, *Dialogue* 60.
[128] Justin Martyr, *First Apology* 63.
[129] Tertullian, *An Answer to the Jews* 9.22-25.

further confirmed by that of Tertullian. We assert, he says, that all the names of a true and proper divinity are common to the Son with the Father and that the Son came in these names, that he acted in these names, and manifested himself to mankind in these names.[130] What moved Moses to ask God for another name, when he had called himself the God of his Fathers, is not our present business to enquire, but it is remarkable that the final letters of Moses question "… what is his Name" (*li mah shemo mah*; vs. 13),[131] make up the most holy and incommunicable Name (YHWH), Jehovah (LORD). And the rabbis have made no small use of it to prove that this Angel of the LORD was the Angel Jehovah, the Memra, the Word.[132]

Job worshiped Christ as God.

That Job, whoever he was, worshiped the true God is most certain, and in no wise to be doubted, if he was a descendent of Abraham by Keturah; and it appears most evident from the LORD's speaking and revealing himself to him, as we find in Job 33:15 and especially 42:5 and also from his being mentioned with Noah and Daniel by the prophet Ezekiel (Ezek 14:14) as a man that knew and feared God.

---

[130] Tertullian, *Against Praxeas*, 17.
[131] De Gols is arguing here that the last letter of each word in Hebrew form the divine name (י ה ו ה).
[132] B. Bibl. In Exodus Occas. Annot II. P. 45.

Some of the ancient Fathers have asserted that Job was a priest of the Most High God, as Abel, Noah, and Melchizedek,[133] and others that he knew God in Trinity and Unity, because he frequently mentions the Spirit of God,[134] and that he knew the Son of God, and worshiped him as such, is to me as plain as a demonstration.

Not to mention therefore what the Christian Fathers have written of him,[135] we have enough for our purpose in the sacred book that goes by his name, and is received in the canon of the Holy Scriptures; and there we find these very remarkable words, "*For I know that my Redeemer lives, and at the last he will stand upon the earth. And after my skin has been thus destroyed, yet in my flesh I shall see God*" (Job 19:25-26). In these few words he expresses his knowledge of, and his faith in his Redeemer. He acknowledges that Redeemer to be God. He owns that there will be a resurrection of the dead and an enjoyment of that God by whom he was redeemed. Very great things in few words, and that made one of the ancients say that no one had spoken so plainly of the resurrection since Christ, as Job had before Christ.[136] And if we compare this with Genesis 49:18 it will agree exactly with Job's expression, "*I have waited for your salvation O LORD.*" And with the

---

[133] Jerome. Ep. Crit. Ad Evangel. Pr. Col. 571.

[134] Job 27:3; 26:13; 33:4.

[135] Augustine, *City of God* 1.18.c.47; Chrysostom, *Homily* 4. *De patient. Job.* See Spanheim's dissertation on Job. Edit. Ludg. Bar. 1703. Tom. 2.

[136] Jerome. Praef. In Job.

weighty truth of the resurrection our Savior tells us of, *"Do not marvel at this, for an hour is coming when all who are in the tombs will hear his voice and come out, those who have done good to the resurrection of life, and those who have done evil to the resurrection of judgment"* (John 5:28-29).

I must further observe that he calls his Savior by the Name of God, which signifies such a Savior as has paid a Price of Redemption (*lutron*); but of this I will say more later.

Job in a word affirms that his Redeemer lives and that he himself shall rise again; which is equivalent to that in the Gospel that *"Christ is the Resurrection and the Life."* St. John could say no more than Job already had. It is Job's hope he is regenerate by it to a lively hope. St. Peter could say no more. He enters into such particulars as *"this flesh and these eyes"* which is as much as was or could be said by St. Paul himself. So that it is plain to a demonstration that Job believed and worshiped Christ as God.

*The Jewish Church in the Wilderness
Worshiped Christ as God.*

I come now to the Jews as a people under a government, having a religion given to them by God himself, as being God's *Peculium*, his Church in the Wilderness.

That this Jewish church in the wilderness worshiped Christ as their God will appear when I shall have shown you,

> *First*, that Christ was the God of the Covenant with the Jews.
> *Second*, that Christ dwelt in the Tabernacle, as God and King of the Jewish church.
> *Third*, that Christ was the Guardian God of Israel in the Wilderness.
> *Fourth*, that they worshiped and adored Christ as their God.
> *Fifth*, that Christ Jesus was the true High-Priest of that church.

First, Christ was the God of the Covenant with the Jewish Church.

That the God who entered into covenant with Abraham and his sons was the Son of God, I have already shown. Now we find Christ performing the promises made to the fathers and receiving them for his own people. He gives them his Law, instructs them in his religion, in that dispensation of it which was to last to the time of reformation; that is, to the time that he himself should *come to his temple* (Mal 3:1), that *God would be manifest in the flesh* (1Ti 3:16), whereupon the worship now erected in the wilderness was both a type and a pledge, shadows of *things to come, the body being Christ* (Col 2:17).

Exodus 19:6. We find the Person entering into this covenant is God, the God who said, "*All the earth is mine,*" or who, in St. Paul's words, "*is over all God blessed forever*" (Rom 9:5), and that is Christ.

Exodus 20. We find this God gave the Law with a majesty fitting the Almighty. Calling himself their God he said, "*I am the LORD your God, Jehovah Elohim, the God Almighty,*" the God of the covenant, the same God who called Moses (Ex 3). That this God was Christ, we have the authority of St. Stephen who says, "*This [Moses] is the one who was in the congregation in the wilderness with the angel who spoke to him at Mount Sinai*" (Acts 7:38).

What Angel was this? He was such a one who was counted worthy to represent the Person, and bear the name of God; for Moses says, "*God spoke all these words*" (Ex 20:1), and the Angel himself assumes that name, "*I am the LORD your God.*" And Moses says, "*Behold, the LORD our God has shown us his glory and greatness, and we have heard his voice out of the midst of the fire. This day we have seen God speak with man, and man still live*" (Deut 5:24). Thus, it is most evident that this Angel who delivered the Law was the Son of God, the Second Person of the Trinity, whose various appearances under the Old Testament were tokens and essays of his incarnation.

Here is a remarkable text. *"Behold, I send an angel before you to guard you on the way and to bring you to the place that I have prepared. Pay careful attention to him and obey his voice; do not rebel against him, for he will not pardon your transgression, for my name is in him"* (Ex 23:20-21). St. Augustine urges this text against Jews and Gentiles in these words,

> Let them diligently search and examine the Scriptures and see if they can find a parallel place where God has said this much of any angel, *"My name is in him."* No, this he only said of the one who brought the people into the Promised Land, and of him only in a view to the changing of his name (Num 13:16). He therefore that said my name is in that Joshua, or Jesus, was himself the true Jesus, governing and leading the people into the Heritage of eternal life, according to the new covenant, of which the old was a figure.[137]

The Jewish doctors say that this Angel was Metatron, the great scribe, the same one Isaiah calls the Counsellor (Isa 9:6), which the LXX call *the Angel of the Great Council.* And Rabbi Moses Nachmanides[138]

---

[137] Augustine, *Against Faustus* 16:19. De Gols seems to take Augustine as saying God put his name into the Angel of the LORD *and also* into Joshua, son of Nun. It is clear from reading this passage in its context that Augustine is saying that the "angel" of Exodus 21 refers to Joshua.
[138] Moses ben Nahman (1194-1270), was commonly called Nachmanides or Ramban. He was a leading medieval Jewish scholar, rabbi, philosopher, physician, kabbalist, and biblical commentator who lived in Spain but was an important figure in the re-establishment of

understands here that Angel of the Covenant, which is spoken of by the prophet Malachi, that is the Messiah. And Maimonides renders this text, "*Behold I send my Word before you.*"[139] Nothing can be plainer than that they themselves understood this to be the Son of God. And when we read that the elders saw the God of Israel (Ex 19:10), we must remember that the invisible Father never exhibited himself to human view and that Christ was therefore that Memra, that Word, which had all along appeared as the God of the covenant.

Let me add only here that Moses Gerund has these words relating to this angel,

> To speak the truth, that Angel is the Angel Redeemer of whom it is written, "*My Name is in him.*" This, I say, is the same Angel who said to Jacob, "*I am the God of Bethel.*" He is also the same Angel of whom it is said, "*and God called to Moses out of the bush;*" and he is called the Angel because he governs the Word. Therefore it is written, "*Jehovah the Lord God brought us out of Egypt;*" and elsewhere, "*he sent his Angel, and brought us out of Egypt.*" Besides, it is written, "*and the Angel of his Face saved them.*" Of this Angel it is also said, "*My Presence shall go before the camp of Israel and shall cause it to rest.*" Lastly, this is the Angel of whom the

the Jewish community in Jerusalem after the crusaders destroyed it in 1099.
[139] Maimonid. more Nevoch. P. 1.c.64.

prophet speaks, "*The Lord whom you seek shall suddenly come to his temple, the Angel of the covenant
whom you desire.*"[140]

The learned Jacobus Alting[141] tells us, from an ancient Jewish catechism,[142] the Hebrew masters say that
in the giving of the Law more than one divine Person
was concerned. For they say that in God is I, You, and
He, which are three Names of three Persons, all which
are invoked on the Feast of Tabernacles: "I, You, and
He, O help us we beseech you." And that to the end
of the Second Commandment the words run in the
first person, and in the third and fourth, in the third
person; from which they argue that the Most High
Spirit spoke the first two commandments, but the rest
were uttered by his Glory, which is the El Shaddai, the
Lord God Almighty; who was known to the fathers,
by whom the prophets spoke, who is called Jah, the
Lord in whom the name of God is; who is the Beloved
of God, who dwells in the temple; who is the Mouth
of the LORD, the Face of the LORD, and the Rock,
and that Goodness which Moses saw when he could
not see God.

---

[140] This is Moses ben Nachman. Cited by Masius, on Joshua 5. Could
be Andreas Masius or the Lutheran Hector Gottfried Masius (1653-
1709).
[141] Jacob Alting (1618-1679). A Dutch philologist and theologian, professor at the University of Groningen.
[142] Alting on Dt 5:6.

This they assert because they say that in God there are three Spirits united together. The lowest of these is the Holy Ghost. The Second is the Intermediate who is called Wisdom and Understanding, and this is the same Spirit who goes forth with water and fire from the middle of the most consummate Glory. The Supreme Spirit is absolutely in silence; and in him all the holy spirits, and in him all the lucid persons consist.

Second, Christ Dwells in the Tabernacle,
as God and King of the Jewish Church.

The Person that had thus entered into covenant with the Jews, commanded Moses, his Prime Minister in State, to build him a tabernacle. *"And let them make me a sanctuary, that I may dwell in their midst"* (Ex 25:8); and *"I will dwell among the people of Israel and will be their God. And they shall know that I am the LORD their God, who brought them out of the land of Egypt that I might dwell among them. I am the LORD their God"* (Ex 29:45-46). When the tabernacle was finished, the same LORD entered it, with a glory and grandeur becoming the eternal majesty of the Son of God, the LORD of Glory. For so we read, *"Then the cloud covered the tent of meeting, and the glory of the LORD filled the tabernacle. And Moses was not able to enter the tent of meeting because the cloud settled on it, and the glory of the LORD filled the tabernacle"* (Ex 40:34-35). For the cloudy pillar which descended, and had previously stood before the door of Moses' tent (Ex 33:9), left now and again, and came here; not standing at the door of it in the form of a pillar, but spreading itself all over the tabernacle, so that it was covered with it (Num 9:15), and filled it within all over at the first consecration.

After this great day, the Glory of the LORD, the Shekinah, retired into the Most Holy Place, within the veil, and resided there over the Ark of the Testimony.[143]

Before I proceed, I must observe here that the Shekinah, the Glory of the LORD, did not only signify a symbol or token of the divine presence by a light or cloud or other glory, but that it signified a divine Person. Rittangel says that the ancient Jews believed the Shekinah not to be the divine Glory, but a divine Person; and that the Targum has frequently rendered it for a Person: and he produces ten places in evidence, and leaves, he says, many more to the reader's observation.[144]

If the Glory of the LORD therefore is a divine Person, and we compare this account with 2Co 6:15-16, it will appear that Christ is that God, that Glory, that divine Person, who dwelt among them. For there the Apostle says, "*What accord has Christ*

---

[143] See Manasse Ben Israel, Concil. Quaest. 44. In Exod.
[144] Rittangel, p. 117.

with Belial? Or what portion does a believer share with an unbeliever? What agreement has the temple of God with idols? For we are the temple of the living God; as God said, 'I will make my dwelling among them and walk among them, and I will be their God, and they shall be my people'" (2Co 6:15-16). These are the very word of God from Leviticus 26:12, and therefore prove Christ to be that very God who dwelt among them. St. John also alludes to this when he says, *"The Word was made flesh and dwelt among us,"* and tabernacled among us (John 1:14).

Further, that Christ presided in the Jewish church as their God and King is evident from these texts compared together:

Isa 60:1. *Arise, shine, for your light has come, and the glory of the LORD has risen upon you.*

Eph 5:14. *Therefore it says, "Awake, O sleeper, and arise from the dead, and Christ will shine on you.*

Now if the LORD Jehovah is not Christ, the prophet is so far from saying that Christ shall give you light that he makes no mention at all of him; and yet St. Paul affirms that it is Christ who gives light. Therefore, that expression, *"The Glory of the Lord has risen upon you,"* is identical with, *"Christ shall give you light."* Christ is therefore that LORD Jehovah, because they are not two different Persons but one and the same here spoken of.

So again, God calls himself the King of Israel; and who that King of Israel is will appear from the description that King gives himself:

Isa 44:6. *Thus says the LORD, the King of Israel and his Redeemer, the LORD of hosts: "I am the first and I am the last; besides me there is no god."*

Rev 22:13. *Therefore "I am the Alpha and the Omega, the first and the last.*

Now there cannot be more than One who is the First and the Last, and the God who calls himself so calls himself the Redeemer, and the King of Israel, and Christ is that First and Last. It therefore follows that he is the God, and King, and Redeemer of Israel.

Again, the same King of Israel is described by the prophet Zechariah in a state of humiliation, as he was by Isaiah in Glory before:

Zech 9:9. *Rejoice greatly, O daughter of Zion! Shout aloud, O daughter of Jerusalem! Behold, your king is coming to you; righteous and having salvation is he, humble and mounted on a donkey, on a colt, the foal of a donkey.*

Mt 21:4-5. *This took place to fulfill what was spoken by the prophet, saying, "Say to the daughter of Zion, 'Behold, your king is coming to you, humble, and mounted on a donkey, on a colt, the foal of a beast of burden.'"*

From comparing these two texts together it appears that the Jewish church had a King, and that he was Christ. Thereupon, the prophet Malachi calls the

temple, which was the palace of the divine King of Israel, the Temple of Christ, *"Behold, I send my messenger,
and he will prepare the way before me. And the Lord whom
you seek will suddenly come to his temple; and the messenger
of the covenant in whom you delight, behold, he is coming,
says the LORD of hosts"* (Mal 3:1). It therefore appears
that Christ is the King of Israel, the LORD of Hosts,
and is that God beside whom there is no other.

*Third, Christ was the Guardian God
of Israel in the Wilderness.*

We have a very particular account of this in Exodus 33. In ch. 32, we find that God plagued Israelites
(vs. 35), who had fallen into the sin of idolatry. Then
we find that God refused to go any longer with them,
but would leave them to the superintendence of an angel (33:2-3). Upon this melancholy news, the people
mourned (vv. 4-6). In vs. 7 we find that God had re-
moved his Presence from the camp. Upon this, Moses
humbly interceded with God not to forsake them (12-
13), and God was intreated (14). *"My Presence shall go
with you."* Moses rejoiced at this, and further begs that
God will be pleased to perform that gracious promise
(15-16). *"If your Presence will not go with me, do not bring
us up from here."* Then God assures Moses that he had
heard him, *"This very thing that you have spoken I will do,*

for you have found favor in my sight, and I know you by name" (Ex 33:17).

Upon the whole, therefore, we find that it was God who conducted Israel in the Wilderness, that God withdrew himself for the sin of the golden calf, that God threatened to leave them, that God promised to send an angel, that Moses prays that God would not give an angel the custody of the people, but that he himself would conduct them in person. God still assures him that an Angel shall accompany him; Moses persistently presses it, that he himself would go with them. Seeing then Moses declared himself so averse to the superintendence of an angel, yet that he who now and all along communed with him was the Person that consented at last to go with the host and govern them himself, it is plain that he must be God—the only begotten God, who called himself I AM, and who showed himself afterward to Moses, as the LORD, the LORD God (34:6), and to whom Moses prayed for pardon, and still interceded for his Presence (9).

We find the further expressed in the history of Balaam (Num 22), where we see that he went to curse the Israelites but was refrained by the Angel of the LORD. Now that this Angel was no less than Jehovah appears from vs. 32 where he tells Balaam, *"Behold, I have come out to oppose you,"* or to be an adversary to you (22), *"because your way is perverse before me,"* for Balaam had done what was contrary to God's command (12).

There we find God said to Balaam, "*You shall not go with them. You shall not curse the people, for they are blessed.*" This is a plain evidence that this God and that Angel were the same Person. But then we find that the Angel of the LORD gave him to leave and go, yet under this constraint, "*Speak only the word that I tell you*" (35). That it was God the Jehovah who put the words in his mouth we find from the following, "*And God met Balaam ... and the LORD put a word in Balaam's mouth*" (23:4-5).

That God Jehovah, and that Angel therefore are one and the same Person is plain to a demonstration. Balaam acknowledges this himself when he says that the appearance of this angel was "*the vision of the Almighty*" (24:4), and further, that this Almighty was Jehovah God, the King of Israel, the God who brought them out of Egypt (23:21-22). These are the very words used by God himself, "*I am the LORD your God who brought you out of the land of Egypt*," and that is Christ.

Fourth, the Jewish Church Worshiped Christ as God.

I have shown before that Christ was the God of the covenant with the Jews. I have shown that Christ dwelt in the Tabernacle as God and King of the Jewish church. I have shown that Christ was the Guardian God of Israel in the wilderness. Now I will show that they worshiped this Christ as God. If I had not one word more to say on this Head, the very premise would produce this consequence, that they worshiped the God of the covenant, that they adored that God to whom they had built a Tabernacle, a moveable temple, and that by his own command, and that they worshiped their God, their Guardian and Defender, with the most solemn worship and adoration. I say, it is natural to believe they worshiped their God that had done such great things for them, and had made them his Peculium, his own people, according to that which God said, "*The people whom I formed for myself that they might declare my praise*" (Isa 43:21).

But however, St. Paul tells us that Christ was the divine Person who was always with the Jews in the wilderness and was both worshiped by them and provoked by them too. For in 1 Corinthians 10 he declares several parts of the divine dispensation such as the cloud, the passage through the Sea, manna, and the water from the Rock, which he says were all transacted by Jesus Christ. At vs. 4 he says expressly, "*And that Rock was Christ.*" Christ was the Supreme Agent, Christ preserved them by the cloud, Christ baptized them in the Sea, Christ led them with manna, Christ gave them drink from the rock. These were the figure and emblem of himself, "*of whose fulness we all receive grace after grace*" (John 1:16).

After that the Apostle relates the sins of the Jews against the very Christ their God. They committed idolatry, they murmured, they committed fornication, and they tempted Christ (vs. 9), they lusted, and received the reward of trespassing against Mercy. As they therefore sinned against him by idolatry, by murmuring, and by lust, so it appears that others who did not join with them in their sins did worship Christ as their God. And the Apostle warns us, from the punishment of those sinners, to worship that God, that Savior, that Jesus in sincerity, that we would not perish as they did who sinned against him. From this argument it is plain that Christ was the God worshiped by the Jews in the wilderness.

In a word, Christ was the end of the law (Rom 10:4). Christ was the body of the ceremonial shadows (Col 2:17). Christ was the center of the prophets (Acts 10:43). Christ is the key of knowledge (Luke 11:52). Christ is all the very spirit and soul of the Old Testament.

Fifth, Christ Jesus the True High-Priest Prefigured by Aaron.

As Jesus Christ was the God and King of the Jews, and dwelt in the tabernacle, and was worshiped as God by the Jews, so he was also prefigured as the *Thanthropos*, God and man, in Aaron the High-Priest.

So Philo the Jew says,[145] that the High-Priest was the type or figure of the only begotten Son of God, who is the eternal High Priest of the vast Temple of the Universe, as he is the Maker therefore.[146]

And when he speaks of his temple clothes, which he says represented the fabric of heaven and earth, he says particularly that the four letters on the front of Aaron's mitre answered to the eternal Being of God. He calls it "the name of the One who is" (*onoma tou ontos*); and says that by it was understood *Jehovah Filius*, God the Son.

Thus, Aaron in his priestly ornaments represented both the divine and human nature of Christ, for the riches of those vestments could signify no clothing, but that of God. His Person as a man represented the antitype of this.

Because he was to sustain the Person of him who was truly God, some privileges were put upon him which supposed him in a manner elevated above the nature of man (Lev 21:10-12). On this, Philo breaks out in these words,

---

[145] Philo. *de Somniis* (*On Dreams*). *Duo gar hiera theou, en men hode ho kosmos en ō kai archiereus ho prōtogonos autou, ho theois logos.* "For there are two temples of God, one [is] this world in which His Firstborn, the divine Word, is high priest." Thanks to Michael Emadi for the following translations.

[146] Ibid. *Logos de estin eikōn theou di' ou sympas ho kosmos edēmiourgeito.* "Now the Word is the image of God through whom the whole world was created."

> The Law will have the High-Priest to partake of
> a nature greater than human, approaching nearer
> to the Divine; or to speak exactly, to be the con-
> fine of both; that men might propitiate God by a
> mediator partaking of both natures, and God by
> using his ministry may reach forth the supplies of
> grace to men.[147]

So clearly is the divinity of Christ prefigured in the Law of Moses; and thus was Aaron a figure of Christ. And thus we may say of him as Baruch said before, "This is our God, and none other shall be accounted of in comparison to him; he has found out all the ways of knowledge, and has given it to Jacob his servant, and to Israel his beloved. Afterward did he show himself upon earth and conversed with men" (Baruch 3:35-37).

It is admirable to consider with what exquisite reason the eternal Logos, who was the Framer of the World, and is as it were invested in his own work, should be the true High-Priest according to the type of Aaron. For who is so fit to be an intercessor with the Father for the offences of the world as he who

---

[147] Philo. *de Monarch. Bouletai gar auton ho nomos meizoons memoipasthai phuseōs ē kat' anthrōpon, engyterō prosionta tēs theeas, methorion, ei dei talēthes legen, amphoin, hina dia mesou tinos anthrōpoi men hilaskōntai theon, theos de tas charitas anthrōpois hypodiakonō tini chrōmenos oregē kai chorēgē.* "For the law intends him to partake of a greater nature than what is customary with mankind being nearer to the divine, that is, on the boarder line. If it is necessary to speak accurately, it is both, so that men may, on the one hand, propitiate God through some mediator, and God, on the other hand, may offer and give his gifts to men by using some subordinate minister."

made it and in whose breast is contained the whole platform? This is he who thoroughly understands the necessities of these and has a perfect knowledge of the frailties and miseries of his creatures. For it is necessary, says Philo, for those who would supplicate the Father of the world,[148] to make use of the Son, the Paraclete, and most consummate in goodness (or in other words, the most compassionate intercessor) for the forgiveness of sins, and the supplies of the most desirable pleasures.

This is very agreeable to what the prophet Zechariah and the Apostle St. Paul say concerning Christ. For the prophet says, *"Behold, the man whose name is the Branch: for he shall branch out from his place, and he shall build the temple of the LORD. It is he who shall build the temple of the LORD and shall bear royal honor and shall sit and rule on his throne. And there shall be a priest on his throne, and the counsel of peace shall be between them both"* (Zech 6:12-13). And St. Paul says, *"So also Christ did not exalt himself to be made a high priest, but was appointed by him who said to him, 'You are my Son, today I have begotten you'"* (Heb 5:5). And again, *"For it was indeed fitting that we should have such a high priest, holy, innocent, unstained, separated from sinners, and exalted above the heavens. He has no need, like*

---

[148] Paraklētō chrēsthai teleiotatō tēn aretēn huiō pros te amnēstian hamartēmatōn kai chorēhian aphthonōtatōn agathōn. "… to regard as *paraklete*, the most perfect Son, in excellence of virtue and that sins may be forgotten and good gifts supplied in abundance."

those high priests, to offer sacrifices daily, first for his own sins and then for those of the people, since he did this once for all when he offered up himself" (Heb 7:26-27). Thus, *"He is able to save to the uttermost those who draw near to God through him, since he always lives to make intercession for them"* (Heb 7:25).

Joshua worshiped Christ as God.

That Joshua the successor of Moses, and the type of the Messiah, worshiped Christ as God, is very plain from Joshua 5:14 where we find these words, *"'No; but I am the commander of the army of the LORD. Now I have come.' And Joshua fell on his face to the earth and worshiped and said to him, 'What does my lord say to his servant?'"* (Josh 5:14).

Now we find that the Person who commanded Moses the same excalceation[149] is there called both LORD, (Jehovah) and God; and by parity of reason, this Captain is that same LORD. As our marginal notes on this place says,[150] in that Joshua worshiped him, he acknowledged him to be God; and in that he calls himself the LORD's Captain, he declares himself to be Christ. For had this certainly not have allowed Joshua to worship him; and had Joshua not known him to be the eternal God, he would never have done it.

---

[149] The act of depriving or divesting of shoes.
[150] These *Notes on the Bible* refer to the Geneva Bible, printed at London (1599), by Christopher Barker (1529-1599).

Christ the God of Israel in Canaan.

Moses had the promise that the Angel would go before the people to bring them into the place which God had prepared (Ex 23:21). This Angel was therefore the Guardian God of Israel in the wilderness, and we have seen before that God was Christ.

Now we find the same Angel, the God of Israel, in Canaan. For we read in Judges 2 that when the Jews were in the Promised Land and had transgressed the divine command, that the same Angel appeared to them and rebuked them at Bochim. Here he declares himself to be that same Angel that brought them from Egypt, and that Angel was God, for he speaks this way, *"Now the angel of the LORD went up from Gilgal to Bochim. And he said, "I brought you up from Egypt and brought you into the land that I swore to give to your fathers. I said, 'I will never break my covenant with you"* (Jdg 2:1). No one but the Almighty God could say this. Then, after he had rebuked them for their sin, and declared to them the penalty (vs. 3), we find how the people were affected with it. *"As soon as the angel of the LORD spoke these words to all the people of Israel, the people lifted up their voices and wept"* (Jdg 2:4). In the next verse, *"They called the name of that place Bochim [that is Weepers] and they sacrificed there to the LORD,"* that Angel, that Christ against whom they had sinned.

Gideon worshiped Christ as God.

That Gideon worshiped Christ as God is so plain that anyone who reads Judges 6 must believe it, or else they must believe that Gideon was an idolater. At vs. 12 we find that, *"The angel of the LORD appeared to him and said to him, 'The LORD is with you, O mighty man of valor'"* (Jdg 6:12). From this is appears that Gideon thought it was a created angel (vs. 13). But when it says, *"Jehovah looked upon him"* (14), it convinced him that he was not a created angel and commissioned him to be a Judge and a Deliverer of Israel. Here we have still the same Person speaking first as an Angel, then as Jehovah, and assuring him of his Presence, *"I will be with you,"* in the same manner as he had done to the Patriarchs before. When Gideon had asked for a token of his Presence, and the Angel had produced a miracle and then departed from him, Gideon said, *"Alas, O LORD God!"* which was not an exclamation through fear or surprise, but was a recognition of his divinity and an act of adoration paid to the divine majesty.

I do freely acknowledge that men have always expressed a very terrible apprehension of present death whenever God decides to appear. Moses was afraid (Ex 3:6). The Israelites prayed that God would not speak to them or else they would die (Ex 20:19). And Manoah said to his wife, *"We shall surely die because we have seen God"* (Jdg 13:22). Even Isaiah said, *"Woe is me, for I am undone* [or cut off], *for my eyes have seen the King, the LORD of Hosts"* (Isa 6:5). If Gideon expressed the same fear, it must be because he has seen God rather than a mere angel.

If it is allowed that his exclamation, *"Alas, I LORD God!"* proceeds from fear, from surprise, and apprehension of present death, it must be allowed at the same time that the Angel was the very God; and this apprehension of death was so strong that God appeared again to remove it. *"Jehovah [The LORD] said to him, 'Peace be to you. Do not fear; you shall not die'"* (Jdg 6:23). This is a confirmation both that his fear was justified and that the Angel whom he had seen was Jehovah—the very God. And then Gideon built an altar there to the LORD, that very LORD who had appeared to him as an Angel, had commissioned him to be a Judge of Israel, and had promised to be with him. He built the altar to him and called it Jehovah Shalom, the LORD Send Peace. This is certainly the highest act of divine worship that a creature can pay to God. That Gideon paid this to Christ is evident, not only because that Angel-Jehovah was the very Christ, but because St. Paul numbers him among the heroes that believed in Christ and worshiped him as the only true God (Heb 11:32).

Manoah worshiped Christ as God.

That Manoah worshiped the Son of God is evident from Judges 13 where we find an Angel appeared, first to his wife, and upon Manoah's prayer (Jdg 13:8-9), the Angel returned again to the woman and Manoah then went and communed with him. Manoah thought all this time that he had been a created angel, until he asked after his name. But that he then believed he was God is apparent, because he promised to worship him. He was confirmed in this opinion when the Angel refused to tell him his name, saying it was a secret, or rather, as in the margin, because it was "wonderful" (18). Upon that, Manoah offered a sacrifice, the Angel standing by who approved of it, "*doing wondrously,*" which is generally interpreted that this Angel Jehovah sent fire from heaven to consume the sacrifice and to confirm their faith his promise. In the flame the Angel ascended, and "*Then Manoah knew that he was the Angel of the LORD*" (Jdg 13:21). This may also be rendered, "*Then Manoah knew that he was the Angel Jehovah.*" That this is the right construction appears from vs. 22 where they expressed their dread, "*We shall surely die because we have seen God.*" From the whole, it spears that Manoah worshiped God, that this God was that Angel, and that this Angel was Christ. So the notes on this place (vs. 11) explain it, he calls him man because he so seemed, but he was Christ the eternal word.[151]

The Prophets worshiped Christ as God.

Our blessed Savior tells us that the things relating to himself were written in Moses, in the Prophets, and in the Psalms (Luke 24:44). St. Peter adds that the Spirit of Christ was in the prophets, who testified beforehand of the sufferings of Christ and of the Glory that should follow (1Pe 1:10-11). Now, can it possibly be conceived that these prophets should by the inspiration of the Holy Spirit of God, speak of all the particulars of the life and death, of the resurrection and ascension of Christ into heaven, and declare these things to the Jews, as the reason of their hope, and not at the same time themselves believe in him? Should they who believed the promise of God, of the Seed of the woman, that first Gospel given to Adam, enlarged to Abraham, and typified by Moses' Law, be ignorant of that Savior whom the Jews looked for and trusted in? At the same time, would they then give and deliver particular revelations concerning him to the Jews, that after ages might know the Messiah by those very particulars which they related of him, and at the same time not believe in him themselves? This I say is inconceivable!

---

[151] Geneva Bible, Note on Jdg 13:11.

It has indeed been questioned by some men of learning whether the prophets had a distinct knowledge of every particular they foretold concerning the Messiah; and who can determine it? Who dares assert it? But that they knew and believed the chief, the principal things relating to the Messiah, this I am very sure of. This I dare boldly to assert and to prove.

They knew the Messiah to be the Son of God, and the Savior of the world. They knew he would appear in the flesh. They knew he would suffer, and that for the sins of mankind. They knew he was to die. They knew he would rise again from the dead. They knew that he by virtue of his death would overcome the Powers of Death, and the Grave. They knew that he would ascend into heaven and sit at the right hand of God. They knew that his Gospel would be preached all over the world, that idolatry would fall before him, and he alone should be adored as the LORD God Almighty, the God of heaven, and the Savior of men. They knew that the Messiah would judge the quick and the dead and that his Kingdom would be an everlasting Kingdom.

Now these are the principal articles of the Christian religion. If I can prove that the prophets knew and believed them, as I am very sure I can, then we may say with the ancients that the Jewish church was the Christian in promise, and the Christian the Jewish church accomplished.[152] Upon this the 7th Article of the Church of England (1571) is grounded which says,

> The Old Testament is not contrary to the New: for both in the Old and New Testament everlasting life is offered to Mankind by Christ, who is the only Mediator between God and Man, being both God and Man. Wherefore they are not to be heard, which feign that the old Fathers did look only for transitory promises.

They are not to be heard who profanely say that Christ was not worshiped by any recorded in the Scriptures.

Let St. Paul be a judge of this matter. *"For I do not want you to be unaware, brothers, that our fathers were all under the cloud, and all passed through the sea, and all were baptized into Moses in the cloud and in the sea, and all ate the same spiritual food, and all drank the same spiritual drink. For they drank from the spiritual Rock that followed them, and the Rock was Christ"* (1Co 10:1-4). Christ led them the entire forty years in the wilderness. Christ was

---

[152] De Gols cites a Greek text in *Answers to the Orthodox Faithful Concerning Some Necessary Questions* (*Quaestiones et Responsiones ad Orthodoxos*), Q. 101. Here is a translation: "Now nothing has separated the gospel from the law as to the manner of its teaching but as to promise and payment it has separated. For what is the law? The gospel announced beforehand. What is the gospel? The law fulfilled."

Older Christians like De Gols attributed this to Justin Martyr, but is almost certainly the work of a later Father, perhaps Theodoret (393 – c. 458/466). See Peter Toth, "New Questions on Old Answers: Towards a Critical Edition of the Answers to the Orthodox of Pseudo-Justin," *Journal of Theological Studies*, NS 65:2 (Oct 2014): 550-599.

their God, their King and Governor. Christ was all in all to them. And yet, for them not to know, nor worship him, who was their Jehovah, their Goel [Redeemer], their Shiloh [Peace], their Emmanuel [God With Us], their Messiah [Christ/Anointed], is a proposition as strange as it is false; so strange that none but such as are deluded by that Spirit of Error which possessed Socinus could have thought so.[153]

Give me leave to lay open their errors a little. The Racovian Catechism has spoken openly and asks this question. "Q. Were not the same promises that are made to us made by the Law of Moses? A. Not any of them; for neither eternal life, nor the Holy Ghost was promised to the obedient by Moses' Law."[154] And that we might know he understood the whole Mosaical dispensation he says in the answer to the 7th Question, that God has reserved the promise of eternal life to the days of the New Testament. And Question 6 he says that supposing any of the ancients were saved, they were saved not by virtue of any of God's promises, but of his abundant goodness, which gave them more than he ever promised them.

Smalcius[155] doubts not to say it is an old wives fable to believe that any of the Fathers of the Old Testament were saved by faith in Christ as Mediator. And

---

[153] Socinians were nontrinitarian in their view of Christ and precursors to many forms of Unitarianism within Protestantism.
[154] *Racovian Catechism* (1605), Ch. 5: Of The Promise of Eternal Life.
[155] Smalcius, c. 4. De bon. oper.

the Racovian Catechism says though none are saved but by faith, this pertains only to the dispensation of the Gospel.[156] To repeat such errors is to refute them, but the falseness has already appeared and will further appear in the following pages.

David worshiped Christ as God.

That David knew and worshiped Christ as God, I think is as plain as the light of the sun.

That he knew God to be Triunal is what several of the Christian writers have asserted,[157] especially from his words, "*By the word of the LORD the heavens were made, and by the breath of his mouth all their host*" (Ps 33:6). Indeed, if he did not mean the Three Persons of the Divinity, it is difficult to find out what he could mean.

But however, he knew and worshiped the Son of God. "*Your throne, O God, is forever and ever. The scepter of your kingdom is a scepter of uprightness; you have loved righteousness and hated wickedness. Therefore God, your God, has anointed you with the oil of gladness beyond your companions*" (Ps 45:6-7); i.e. God has made your both

---

[156] *Racovian Catechism*, Ch. 11: Of Justification.
[157] A large catalog of Fathers in Daniel Waterland, "Christ Properly Creator: or Christ's Divinity Proved from Creation, The Second Sermon Preached Oct. 7, 1719," in *The works of The Rev. Daniel Waterland, D. D.* 2nd ed. vol. 2, ed. William Van Mildert, D. D. (Oxford: University Press, 1843), 49-67. Daniel Cosgrove Waterland (1683 – 1740), was an English theologian, Chancellor of the Diocese of York and Archdeacon of Middlesex.

Lord and Christ. And that this was spoken of Christ
we have St. Paul's authority (Heb 1:8), and the Targum also, which perhaps may be of greater authority
with our adversaries.[158]

Again, the same Psalmist says, *"The LORD* [Yah-
weh/Jehovah] *says to my Lord* [Adonai]: *'Sit at my right
hand, until I make your enemies your footstool'"* (Ps 110:1).
Our Savior himself produces this text as a proof of his
Divinity and of David's knowing him to be God. This
scene with Christ is of such importance that it is recorded by three Evangelists (Matt 22:44; Mark 12:36;
Luke 20:42). The Apostles also have made use of this
text as a testimony of Christ's Divinity and his ascension into heaven (Acts 2:34). Even some of the most
learned Jews acknowledge that this Psalm is spoken of
the Messiah.[159]

David not only worshiped Christ as God himself
but called upon all true Israelites to join with him in
the adoration. *"I will tell of the decree: The LORD said to
me, 'You are my Son; today I have begotten you'"* (Ps 2:7).
At vs. 8, he speaks of the glory of his kingdom, and
talks of his power, and declares that he will be hon-
ored by all the kings and princes of the earth.

---

[158] It is difficult to know what De Gols means by including the Targum
here, for he does not elaborate. It could be simply that the Targum
calls this king "God." It could also be that some versions of the Targum
refer to "the throne of your Glory, O LORD," where the Shekinah-
Glory acts like the Memra and is therefore Christ.
[159] See Rabbi Saadia (882/892 – 942), cited by Grotius, Rel. Ch. 1.5. §
22. No. 1.

Thereupon he says, *"Kiss the Son, lest he be angry"* (12). The adoration is not only required, but the reasons and motives are added. The reason is because he is the Son. St. Paul proves this in Hebrews 1 when he shows that he is the eternal Son of the eternal God. David calls him Jehovah, *"Serve the LORD with fear and rejoice with trembling"* (Psalm 2:11). Then he adds the motives. First, from the penalty, *"Lest you perish."* Next, from the benefit of his service, *"Blessed are all who put their trust in him."*

That divine worship and religious adoration is signified by *"kiss,"* will appear when I shall have shown you how a kiss was used as an act of divine worship and part of solemn adoration by almost all the nations of the world.

Of a kiss in religious worship.

That by the word "kiss" is understood an act of divine adoration, including all the acts of worship, of honor, prayer, thanksgiving, and service, will appear from the general use of that outward action, to declare all inward veneration and express all obedience.

So we find it: *"Yet I will leave seven thousand in Israel, all the knees that have not bowed to Baal, and every mouth that has not kissed him"* (1Kg 19:18). Also, *"And now they sin more and more, and make for themselves metal images ... It is said of them, 'Those who offer human sacrifice kiss calves!'"* (Hos 13:2).

Job tells us of the idolaters that worshiped the Sun and Moon, and that because they could not reach them, they lifted up their hands to them. They kissed their hands in demonstration of the most solemn worship and then held their hands up to them, as it were, to throw that kiss to them, which they would give them if they were within their reach. Thus, he says, *"If I have looked at the sun when it shone, or the moon moving in splendor, and my heart has been secretly enticed, and my mouth has kissed my hand"* (Job 31:26-27). And that Job understood by this kissing of the hand that the most solemn act of divine adoration and religious worship is evident from vs. 28, here he says it is open idolatry, *"This also would be an iniquity to be punished by the Judge, for I would have denied the God above"* (Job 31:28).

The word "adoration," which we use for the highest act of divine worship, signifies "to put the hand to the mouth." It is derived from this religious custom. Pliny says that in worship we put the right hand to the mouth.[160] Apuleius describes the manner of it among the Romans.[161] Lucian[162] among the Indians and Demosthenes for the Greeks say that except

---

[160] Pliny, 1.20.c.2. *In adorando dextram ad osculum referimus.*
[161] Apuleius, 1.4. Asin. Aur.
[162] Lucian. 1. "When they arise in the morning they worship the sun, kissing their hand."

for when the idol or deity was out of their reach, they otherwise kissed the idol. Cicero tells us of a brazen statue of Hercules, whose jaws and chin were worn away by the worshipers who kissed it, because they were prone not only to pray to it, but to kiss it also.[163]

But let me now return to David. That he knew the Son of God would become flesh and appear in human nature is certain from Psalm 40:6-8. That this Psalm does pertain to Christ and speak of his incarnation for our redemption, St. Paul assures us, since he is certainly the best interpreter and in whose words we rind, "*Consequently, when Christ came into the world, he said, 'Sacrifices and offerings you have not desired, but a body have you prepared for me; in burnt offerings and sin offerings you have taken no pleasure. Then I said, 'Behold, I have come to do your will, O God, as it is written of me in the scroll of the book.' When he said above, 'You have neither desired nor taken pleasure in sacrifices and offerings and burnt offerings and sin offerings' (these are offered according to the law), then he added, 'Behold, I have come to do your will.' He does away with the first in order to establish the second. And by*

---

[163] For more see Pierre Danet, "Adorare," in *A Complete Dictionary of the Greek and Roman Antiquities Explaining the Obscure Places in Classic Authors and Ancient Historians Relating to the Religion, Mythology, History, Geography and Chronology of the Ancient Greeks and Romans, Their … Rites and Customs, Laws, Polity, Arts and Engines of War: Also an Account of Their Navigations, Arts and Sciences and the Inventors of Them: With the Lives and Opinions of Their Philosophers / Compiled Originally in French … by Monsieur Danet; Made English, with the Addition of Very Useful Mapps,* Early English Books Online (London: Printed for John Nicholson … Tho. Newborough … and John Bulford .., 1700).

that will we have been sanctified through the offering of the body of Jesus Christ once for all" (Heb 10:5-10). This is to the point; God can assume a human body. This is not only agreeable to his almighty power, and not contrary to our reason to believe, but is acknowledged not only by the Talmud, but by Rabbi Solomon, as Grotius tells us.[164]

Further, David believed that Christ, the Messiah, was to suffer. In Psalm 22 he describes several particulars of his Passion. That they do pertain to Christ, we must believe from the Evangelists. For,

Psalm 22	The NT
Vs. 1. *My God, my God, why have you forsaken me?*	Mt 27:46. *And about the ninth hour Jesus cried out with a loud voice, saying, "Eli, Eli, lema sabachthani?" that is, "My God, my God, why have you forsaken me?"*
Vv. 7-8. *All who see me mock me; they make mouths at me; they wag their heads;*	Mt 27:39. *And those who passed by derided him, wagging their heads.*
"He trusts in the LORD; let him deliver him; let him rescue him, for he delights in him!"	Mt 27:43. *He trusts in God; let God deliver him now, if he desires him.*
Vs. 16. *They have pierced my hands and feet.*	Mt 27:35. *And when they had crucified him,*

[164] Grotii Ver. Christ. Rel. 1. 5. § 21. no. 9.

| Vs. 18. They divide my gar-ments among them, and for my clothing they cast lots. | they divided his garments among them by casting lots. (see also Luke 23:34) |
| Vs. 22. I will tell of your name to my brothers; in the midst of the congregation I will praise you. | Heb 2:12. I will tell of your name to my brothers; in the midst of the congregation I will sing your praise. |

From all these places it is evident that this Psalm relates to Christ, speaks of Christ, and was fulfilled in Christ. For to believe that all this was accidental only is to deny a providence. More, it is to deny the Evangelists themselves who acknowledge that these things were done that it might be fulfilled which was spoken by the prophet (Matt 27:35), and that the Scripture might be fulfilled (John 19:24, 37), which both refer to this very Psalm.

David believed and spoke of Christ's death and resurrection. *"For you will not abandon my soul to Sheol, or let your holy one see corruption"* (Ps 16:10). That the prophet spoke this of Christ, St. Peter assures us, *"Brothers, I may say to you with confidence about the patriarch David that he both died and was buried, and his tomb is with us to this day. Being therefore a prophet, and knowing that God had sworn with an oath to him that he would set one of his descendants on his throne, he foresaw and spoke about the resurrection of the Christ, that he was not abandoned to Hades, nor did his flesh see corruption"* (Acts 2:29-31).

David believed and spoke of Christ's ascension into heaven and the outpouring of the Holy Ghost, and that he was prepared a place in heaven for them that worship him here below. *"You ascended on high, leading a host of captives in your train and receiving gifts among men, even among the rebellious, that the LORD God may dwell there. Blessed be the Lord, who daily bears us up; God is our salvation. Selah. Our God is a God of salvation, and to GOD, the Lord, belong deliverances from death"* (Ps 68:18-20). What could any Christian add to this or profess more plainly? And how St. Paul applies this to Christ, we find in Ephesians 4:8. That it does belong to Christ is certain; for either Christ must be the Person of whom the Psalmist speaks, or St. Paul must grossly misquote and misapply him. If he is the same Person, then from that Psalm it is evident:

- That Christ went before the people and marched with them through the wilderness (Ps 68:7-15).
- That it was Christ who was among the thousands of angels in Sinai, in the holy place, and by their ministry gave the Law (vs. 17).
- That Christ was the God and King, whose goings were seen in the sanctuary (vs. 24).
- That it was Christ who was the God of the temple at Jerusalem (vs. 29).

All these things are expressly spoken of him who ascended on high, and led captivity captive, and received gifts for men; and the Apostle says that this was Christ.

Lastly, David believed Christ to be the Judge of all the world. This appears in his excellent prayer, *"May God be gracious to us and bless us and make his face to shine upon us, Selah. That your way may be known on earth, your saving power among all nations. Let the peoples praise you, O God; let all the peoples praise you! Let the nations be glad and sing for joy, for you judge the peoples with equity and guide the nations upon earth"* (Ps 67:1-4). What Christian could have made a more excellent prayer or more agreeable to what our Savior taught us, *"Hallowed be your Name, your Kingdom come?"* What Christian could have made a truer confession of faith in Christ than this one from David? And therefore, to assert that David knew nothing of Christ, and never worshiped him, is a piece of amazing impudence.

Solomon worshiped Christ as God.

That Solomon worshiped Christ as God is certain, for he was instructed in the religion of his father David; and he has given us such descriptions of the Son of God as must convince us that he both knew and adored him as God.

As soon as Solomon was born, *"The LORD loved him"* (2Sa 12:24). In demonstration of that love, God sent Nathan the prophet to call him Jedidia, i.e.

Beloved of God, or beloved because of God, or beloved for the sake of God, for Christ's sake, in whom he was acceptable to God, and of whose Glory and Kingdom he was a type and figure.[165] Indeed, he was so beloved of God that God said, *"He shall be my son, and I will be his Father"* (1Ch 22:9).

This man, according to God's own appointment, built a temple to God and consecrated it with a most excellent prayer, even to that God who was the God of the covenant—Christ Jesus. Christ's Ark, the visible token of the covenant, and figure of the body of Christ, was placed inside. How acceptable both the temple and consecration was appears from the gracious answer God gave. *"Now my eyes will be open and my ears attentive to the prayer that is made in this place. For now I have chosen and consecrated this house that my name may be there forever. My eyes and my heart will be there for all time"* (2Ch 7:15-16). Then the Shekinah, the Glory of the LORD, which is Christ, he himself dwelt there and filled the house with a cloud. He took possession of it as his palace, with a pomp and magnificence becoming the God and King of the Jews (1Kg 8:10), as he had done to the tabernacle before.

This Solomon speaks of the Son of God, and of his eternal Generation before the creation of the world (Prov 8:22-32), and then closes that description with these words, *"And now, O sons, listen to me: blessed*

---

[165] Junius-Tremellius Bible (1575), in the place cited.

are those who keep my ways" (Prov 8:32), which Christ Jesus, his Antitype, expressed when he said, *"Blessed rather are those who hear the word of God and keep it!"* (Luke 11:28).

For that the Wisdom of God, so often mentioned, and so much celebrated by Solomon, does not signify the essential property of the divine Nature, his knowledge and understanding, but the Person of the Son of God, the Lord Jesus Christ, is beyond all doubt. This is because Christ is called the Wisdom of God (Luke 11:49). That Christ must be understood there, is plain in the parallel when it says, *"I will send to you prophets and wise men"* (Matt 23:34), which the Wisdom of God in the other place is said to send. St. Paul gives us the reason why he is called the Wisdom of God. *"In him are hidden all the treasures of wisdom and knowledge"* (Col 2:3).

This text of Solomon's is a strong argument for the divinity of this personal Wisdom, though Arius made use of it against Christ, because the LXX had rendered the Hebrew "possessed me" (*qanani*), with "created me" (*ektisen me*), instead of "possessed me" (*ektēse me*). But the original is to be our guide, and that has it from the root "to possess, to enjoy in possession" (*qanah*). Aquila has rendered it with the affix, as it is in the Hebrew "he possessed me" (*ektēsato me*); although the other word might bear a good construction with those who are not heretically minded.[166]

And of this Wisdom he says that he is eternal, is equal with God, is of God, is the Creator of all things, always was, and always is with the Father; and that he is the Blessing of God to mankind, is their God and Guide here, and their Glory and Salvation hereafter.

Further, at vs. 31 Solomon speaks of his incarnation, *"Rejoicing in his inhabited world and delighting with the children of man"* (Prov 8:31), which Baruch, speaking of the same Wisdom, explains, "Afterward he showed himself upon earth, and conversed with men" (Baruch 3:37).

Proverbs 30:4 speaks of the Son of God in these words, *"Who has ascended to heaven and come down? Who has gathered the wind in his fists? Who has wrapped up the waters in a garment? Who has established all the ends of the earth? What is his name, and what is his son's name? Surely you know!"* In these words Solomon asserts the omnipotence both of God the Father and God the Son; and plainly acquaints us that he knew the Son of God and adored him too.[167] This is so evident that the Jewish masters of old believed that Wisdom and this Son were the same—either the Word or the Spirit, but generally the former.[168]

---

[166] See Zanch. Trib. Elohim 1. 3. C. 8. P. 470.
[167] Remus in Proverbs 30. De Gols seems to refer to Georg Remus (1561-1625).
[168] Peter Allix, *Judgment of the Jewish Church.*

Even more, Solomon made his prayers to the Son of God, to Christ. This appears in Proverbs 30:1. The prayer we have is in vv. 7-9, but the object of that invocation is in vs. 1, "*The man spoke to Ithiel and Ucal.*"[169] These are two names given to the Son of God, answering to Emmanuel. For Ithiel signifies "*My Strong God,*" or The Powerful God is With Me; and Ucal, a word which signifies ability, is, my God Who is Able to Save Me. This is explained by Isaiah 9:6, "*The Mighty God.*" And what that mighty God is to mankind we find in St. Paul. "*Because of him you are in Christ Jesus, who became to us Wisdom from God, Righteousness and Sanctification and Redemption*" (1Co 1:30).

Lastly, this very Solomon confessed his belief of a future judgment and warned others of it (Ecc 11:9). Therefore, for the Socinians to say that he knew not the Son of God is as false as it was rash for Cardinal Bellarmine to say that Solomon was forsaken of God and reprobated.[170] For though Solomon sinned greatly, yet there is reason to believe he repented sincerely, from his book of Ecclesiastes, and that this very book was a demonstration of it (Ecc 7:23, etc.). Neither can it be deemed otherwise. Rather, it is exceedingly rash to judge such a person, whom God had made a type of his Son and an author of such books as

---

[169] The ESV translates this as, "*The man declares, I am weary, O God; I am weary, O God, and worn out.*" The NAS follows the KJV, however, choosing to interpret these words as names.

[170] Bellarm. De verb. Dei, 1. 1. C. 5.

are the canon of Salvation to others, to judge such a person a cast-away. God had promised, *"When he commits iniquity, I will discipline him with the rod of men, with the stripes of the sons of men, but my steadfast love will not depart from him"* (2Sa 7:14-15). From this text and 2 Chronicles 11:17, where the way of David and Solomon are mentioned with honor, the ancient Jews have concluded and asserted that he did repent.[171]

Isaiah worshiped Christ as God.

I come now to the prophet Isaiah, whom Jesu Sirach calls the Great Prophet (Ecclesiasticus 48:22). He was a great prophet indeed, in every respect, but more especially in regard to his knowledge and description of the Messiah, the Son of God, and the Savior of the world; whose life and death he described not as a prophet but an historian, not as a prophecy to come, but as a fact already past. Thus, St. Jerome[172] does not doubt to call this Isaiah both an Evangelist and Apostle; and St. Athanasius[173] says that the greatest part of his prophecy is the Gospel concerning the coming of the Word of God in the flesh, and of the sufferings he underwent for our sakes.

This Isaiah is the great morning-star, shining through the veil of Moses' types, and foreshadowing

---

[171] Ravanel. Bibl. P. 637.
[172] Jerome, in Proaem. In If.
[173] Athanasius, in Synopsi.

the rising of the Sun of Righteousness. To mention all that he knew and believed of the Son of God, and how he worshiped him as God and Savior, would be to transcribe him. I shall mention only a few particulars.

That Isaiah knew the Trinity of Persons in the Unity of the Divine Nature is more than probable because he names them most distinctly and ascribes personal attributes and operations to them. He says, *"I will recount the steadfast love of the LORD, the praises of the LORD, according to all that the LORD has granted us"* (Isa 63:7). Whether there is any force in the three-fold repeating of the word Jehovah, I take not upon me to determine. But I am very sure there is just two verses later. *"In all their affliction he was afflicted, and the angel of his presence saved them; in his love and in his pity he redeemed them; he lifted them up and carried them all the days of old. But they rebelled and grieved his Holy Spirit"* (Isa 63:9-10). Here, the Son and Spirit are distinctly named, and both act as Persons distinct from the Father.

But however that is, it is certain that Isaiah knew the Messiah to be God, to be the Son of God, and adored him as such. For so we find from his own words, *"I saw the Lord sitting upon a throne, high and lifted up; and the train of his robe filled the temple. Above him stood the seraphim ... And one called to another and said: 'Holy, holy, holy is the LORD of hosts; the whole earth is full of his glory!' ... And I said: 'Woe is me! For I am lost; for I am a*

*man of unclean lips ... for my eyes have seen the King, the
LORD of hosts!"* (Isa 6:1-5).

Now who this LORD of Hosts was, whom
Isaiah saw, St. John tells us; it is Christ. For he says,
*"Isaiah said these things because he saw his glory and spoke
of him"* (John 12:41). And what St. John quotes from
the prophet of the judicial hardness that should befall
the Jews is taken from vv. 9-10 of that chapter of
Isaiah.

If we compare this text with Revelation 4:8, we
find this same Glory given to God the Father. From
this it necessarily follows that Christ is of the same nature, honor, and glory with the Father, the same
LORD of Hosts, the same eternal God. Or, we must
believe that Isaiah and the Evangelist have robbed the
Father of his Honor and given it to another, to whom
it was not due. And here I am further to observe that
the seraphim, by crying to each other, did not only
declare the nature of God, and recognize his authority
over all the world, but did solemnly invoke and worship him as that God , who is most holy, and by whom
they are and were created.

Again, Isaiah calls Christ the Immanuel, which is
the chief name of the Messiah, having relation to the
divine and human natures in the hypostatic union,
Christ, God and man (Isa 7:14 and 8:8), which was the
name given by the angel. *"They shall call his name Immanuel, which means, 'God with us'"* (Matt 1:23).

Again, Isaiah calls Christ by the name of Goel, the Redeemer, "*And the Redeemer shall come to Zion*" (Isa 59:20).

Goel, Redeemer.

Here I find myself obliged to explain the word, because I find there is very great stress laid upon it in the holy Scriptures, and because it has been observed[174] that this word is used more than six hundred times in the Old Testament, for such a Redeemer as the New Testament describes Jesus Christ to be.

The word *goel* signifies one allied or related in blood. Thus, it is rendered "a relation" (*propinquus*). Thus, Christ, who took upon him the Seed of Abraham, is not ashamed to call us brothers, so the Apostle tells us, "*For he who sanctifies and those who are sanctified all have one source. That is why he is not ashamed to call them brothers*" (Heb 2:11). The Apostle confirms this with a prophecy of David's (Ps 22:22), that the Savior should call his redeemed "brothers."

Again, Goel signifies a person who has the right of inheritance (Lev 25:25), and not a right only, but a power also, to vindicate his right. Thus, Christ is so called, because he has a right to have the heathen for

---

[174] Fredrick Spanheim. Dissert. De Jobo, p. 108. Tom. Ii. Lug. Bat. 1703.

his inheritance, and the utmost parts of the earth for his possession (Ps 2:8).

And again, Goel is such a redeemer as has paid a ransom, a price of redemption.

That a ransom, a *lutron*, was necessary for our redemption, Job was not ignorant of; for these are his words, "*If there be for him an angel, a mediator, one of the thousand, to declare to man what is right for him, and he is merciful to him, and says, 'Deliver him from going down into the pit; I have found a ransom'*" (Job 33:23-24), or an atonement, as it is in the margin note. And David says, "*Truly no man can ransom another, or give to God the price of his life, for the ransom of their life is costly and can never suffice*" (Ps 49:7-8). It also seems that Jacob, before them both, knew and understood the redemption by a ransom; for he uses this very word when he calls the Son of God, "*The Angel who redeemed me*" (Gen 48:16). And Aben Ezra, expounding Isaiah 59:20. "*And the Redeemer shall come to Zion,*" acknowledges this Redeemer to be one who must pay the price of redemption.

And so, the New Testament describes Christ as that Redeemer who has paid for our redemption. "*Christ gave his life a ransom for many*" (Matt 20:28). "*God has purchased his Church with his own blood*" (Acts 20:28). "*For there is one God, and one Mediator between God and man, the Man Christ Jesus, who gave himself a ransom for all*" (1Ti 2:5-6). "*For you are bought with a price"* (1Co 6:20). *"For as much as you know that you were not redeemed with corruptible things, like silver and gold … but with the precious blood of Christ, the Lamb without blemish or spot"* (1Pe 1:18-19).

To return to Isaiah, as he knew the Messiah the Son of God to be the Redeemer, so he has given a most particular account of the sufferings he underwent to perfect that redemption, in the fifty-third chapter of his prophecy, where he describes the Messiah in the state of humiliation, his sorrows, sufferings, death, and burial; and also the state of his glorification. The particulars are so lively and so perfect that whosoever reads that chapter attentively must think it to be something a Gospel writer described rather than a prophet predicting the suffering of a Person to come. Thus, several of the greatest masters of the Jews have acknowledged that this chapter related entirely to the Messiah.[175]

What Isaiah believed and wrote of Christ the Son of God we have seen before. What the other prophets knew and believed, this would take a whole volume to describe. Thus, I could say much. Whatever the Gospel of Christ has taught us, One or another of the prophets have known, revealed, and believed. Whatever the Apostles preached of Jesus Christ and the power of his resurrection, the prophets have known

---

[175] See the Targum and Gemara of Babylon. Grotius, Rel. Ch. Verit. 1. 5. § 19. And Rivet. In Isa 53:4.

and revealed, not all at once, as it is delivered to us, but by degrees, plainer and clearer, as Christ the Sun of Righteousness drew nearer and nearer to his rising to this world (Acts 3:24).

Glossary of Works and Authors Cited

There are many obscure and long since forgotten authors and works cited in De Gol's discussions on Christ and the Angel. This Appendix contains a short biography of many of these men and some of those works.

AGRIPPA HENRY, CORNELIUS (1486-1535). German polymath, physician, legal scholar, soldier, theologian, and occult writer. Later rejected his book *Occult Philosophy*.

AINSWORTH, HENRY (1571-1622). English Nonconformist clergyman and scholar.

ALTING, JACOBUS (1618-1679). A Dutch philologist and theologian, professor at the University of Groningen.

AMBROSE OF MILAN (333–397). Bishop of Milan and teacher of Augustine who defended the divinity of the Holy Spirit and the perpetual virginity of Mary.

ATHANASIUS OF ALEXANDRIA (c. 295–373; fl. 325–373). Bishop of Alexandria from 328, though often in exile. He wrote his classic polemics against the Arians while most of the eastern bishops were against him.

AUGUSTINE (354–430). Bishop of Hippo and a voluminous writer on philosophical, exegetical, theological and ecclesiological topics. In the West, he towers over all others.

BARKER, CHRISTOPHER (1529-1599). Printer to Queen Elizabeth. Printed the Geneva Bible and its notes.

BASIL THE GREAT (329-79). One of the Cappadocian fathers, bishop of Caesarea and champion of the teaching on the Trinity propounded at Nicaea in 325. He was a great administrator and founded a monastic rule.

BELLARMINE, ROBERT (1542 –1621). Italian Jesuit and Cardinal. He was an important figure in the Counter-Reformation and a proponent of the Council of Trent.

BEZA, THEODORE (1519-1605). French Reformed Protestant theologian, disciple of John Calvin, successor to Calvin as the spiritual leader of Geneva.

BULL, GEORGE (1634-1710). English theologian, Bishop of St. David's. Wrote a work on the Creed and defended the Trinity against heretics.

BUXTORF (1564-1629). Johannes Bustorf. Hebraist, professor of Hebrew at Basel (Switzerland), known as "Master of the Rabbis." (PA)

CELSUS (2nd Cent. AD). Greek philosopher and opponent of Christianity.

CHRYSOSTOM, JOHN (344/354–407; fl. 386–407). Bishop of Constantinople who was noted for his orthodoxy, his eloquence and his attacks on Christian laxity in high places.

CLARKE, SAMUEL (1675-1729). Socinian and anti-Trinitarian leader of the Enlightenment. He believed that Christ was merely a man.

CLEMENT OF ALEXANDRIA (c. 150–215). A highly educated Christian convert from paganism, head of the catechetical school in Alexandria and pioneer of Christian scholarship.

CUNÆUS, PETRUS (1586-1638). Peter van der Kun. Dutch Christian Rabbinical scholar at the University of Leyden.

CYPRIAN (200-258). Martyred bishop of Carthage who maintained that those baptized by schismatics and heretics had no share in the blessings of the church.

CYRIL OF ALEXANDRIA (375–444). Patriarch of Alexandria whose extensive exegesis and strong view of the unity of Christ led to the condemnation of Nestorius in 431.

DRUSIUS (1550-1616). Johannes van den Driesche. Flemish Protestant divine, Orientalist, Christian Hebraist, and exegete; speculated about the existence of 1 Enoch.

EPIPHANIUS OF SALAMIS (310-403 A.D). Bishop of Salamis, Cyprus, defender of the orthodox faith against various heresies.

ERASMUS, DESIDERIUS (1466-1536). Dutch Catholic "Prince of the Humanists," his work in the New Testament raised important questions for the Reformers, but he himself remained loyal to Rome.

EUSEBIUS OF CAESAREA (c. 260/263–340). Bishop of Caesarea, partisan of the Emperor Constantine and first historian of the Christian church.

FAGIUS, PAUL (1504-49). Renaissance scholar of Biblical Hebrew and Protestant Reformer.

GALE, THEOPHILUS (1628-1678). English Puritan educationalist, nonconformist, and theologian of dissent.

GOSLAVIUS, ADAM (1577-1642). 17th century Socinian pupil of Nicholas Taurelli. He was a Polish Knight from Bebeln, Germany and had a brother named Andrew who was also a Socinian.

GREGORY OF NAZIANZUS (b. 329/330; fl. 372–389). Cappadocian father, bishop of Constantinople, friend of Basil the Great and Gregory of Nyssa, and author of theological orations, sermons and poetry.

GREGORY OF NYSSA (c. 335–394). Bishop of Nyssa and brother of Basil the Great. A Cappadocian father and author of catechetical orations, he was a philosophical theologian of great originality.

GREGORY, JOHN (1607-1646). English orientalist, he wrote *Notes and Observations upon some Passages of Scripture* (1646).

GROTIUS, HUGO (1583-1645). Dutch Jurist and Arminian theologian, he is noted for his "governmental" or "moral government" theory of the atonement and for being imprisoned for his views.

HEYLIN, PETER (1599-1662) English ecclesiastic and author of many works, including one on the Apostle's Creed.

HILARY OF POITIERS (c. 315–367). Bishop of Poitiers and called the "Athanasius of the West" because of his defense (against the Arians) of the common nature of Father and Son.

HOORNBECK, JOHANNES (1617-1666). Dutch Reformed theologian, pupil of Voetius; moved to Germany to pastor a refugee Reformed church in Mulheim. Later became professor at Leiden. Wrote important works on missions.

IRENAEUS OF LYONS (c. 135–c. 202). Bishop of Lyons who published the most famous and influential refutation of Gnostic thought.

JEROME (c. 347–420). Gifted exegete and exponent of a classical Latin style, now best known as the translator of the Latin Vulgate. He defended the perpetual virginity of Mary, attacked Origen and Pelagius and supported extreme ascetic practices.

JUNIUS-TREMELLIUS BIBLE (1575). Immanuel Tremellius (1510-80) was an Italian Jewish convert to Christianity, a leading Hebraist and Bible translator. Franciscus Junius was his son-in-law and together they worked on a Latin translation of the Bible from the Hebrew and Syriac.

JUSTIN MARTYR (100/110–165). Palestinian philosopher who was converted to Christianity. He traveled to Rome and wrote several apologies (defenses of the faith) against both pagans and Jews; he was eventually martyred.

KABBALAH. Esoteric method, discipline, and school of thought of Judaism. The **Zohar** (13th cent. but with oral tradition dating back to untold primordial time) is one of the main texts of Kabbalah.

LEO THE GREAT (regn. 440–461). Bishop of Rome whose *Tome to Flavian* helped to strike a balance between Nestorian and Cyrilline positions at the Council of Chalcedon in 451.

LETTER OF SIX BISHOPS (268 AD). Or *Letter of Hymenaeus*. Letter elaborating the received catechetical tradition of Christ in the Old Testament, directed at the heretic Paul of Samosata. Soon led to the synod of seventy elders.

Lightfoot, John (1602-1675). English churchman, rabbinical scholar, Vice-Chancellor at the University of Cambridge. Wrote the important work *A Commentary on the New Testament from the Talmud and Hebraica*.

MAIMONIDES (1135-1204). Moses ben Maimon. Spanish born rabbi who become one of the most influential of all medieval Torah scholars.

MANASSEH BEN ISRAEL (1604-1657). Manoel Dias Soeiro. Portuguese rabbi, kabbalist, printer and publisher.

MARCKII, JOHANNIS (1656-1731). Johannes a Marck. Dutch Reformed theologian and church historian who the book *Compendium theologiæ Christianæ.*

MASIUS, ANDREAS (1514-73). Catholic priest, humanist, and one of the first Europeans to specialize in the Syriac language.

MILL, JOHN (1645-1707). English theologian who wrote a critical edition of the Greek New Testament with notes on over thirty-thousand variants.

MORE, HENRY (1614-1687). English philosopher and Rationalist of the Cambridge Platonist school.

MOSES GERUND. See **Moses Ben Nachman.**

MOSES BEN NAHMAN (1194-1270). Commonly called Nachmanides or Ramban or Moses ben Nachman Gerondi (Moses Gerundensis). Leading medieval Jewish scholar, rabbi, philosopher, physician, kabbalist, and biblical commentator. He lived most of his life in Girona, Catalonia (Spain).

MOSES BEN MAIMON. See **Maimonides.**

NOETUS (fl. 230 AD). Presbyter in Asia Minor and proponent of the heresy called modalistic Monarchianism or Patripassianism.

NOVATIAN OF ROME (fl. 235–258). Roman theologian, otherwise orthodox, who formed a schismatic church after failing to become pope. His treatise on the Trinity states the classic Western doctrine.

ORIGEN (b. 185; fl. c. 200–254). Influential exegete and systematic theologian from Alexandria, Egypt. He was condemned (perhaps unfairly) for maintaining the preexistence of souls while purportedly denying the resurrection of the body. His extensive works of exegesis focus on the spiritual meaning of the text.

PARKER, SAMUEL (1681-1730). Nonjuror (declined oaths of allegiance) and theological writer, bishop of Oxford, wrote *Bibliotheca*

Biblica, a *Patristic Commentary on the Scriptures* (1720-35). It only covered the Pentateuch.

PEARSON, JOHN (1613-1686). English theologian and scholar. Wrote a work in the Creed that mined the Church Fathers.

PERKINS, WILLIAM (1558-1602). English Puritan theologian and leader of the Puritan movement in the Church of England during Elizabeth's reign.

PHILO (20 BC – 50 AD). Alexandrians Jewish Hellenistic philosopher who lived during the time of Christ, he is one of the best monotheistic proponents who believed in a "second God" called the Logos, which lends itself nicely towards an understanding of Christ in the OT.

RACOVIAN CATECHISM (1605). A Socinian catechism meant to destroy the Gospel.

RAVANELLUS, PETRUS (d. 1680). Published *Bibliothica Sacra, seu Thesaurus Scripturea*. Geneva, 1654.

REMUS, GEORG (1561-1625). German lawyer, philologe, historian, poet. Vice Chancellor at the University of Jena.

RIDDERUS, FRANCISCUS (1618-1683). Dutch Reformed minister who served at Schermorhorn, Brielle, and Rotterdam. He wrote religious poems and devotional books.

RITTANGEL, JOHANN STEPHAN (1602-1652). German Jew who converted to Roman Catholicism, then became a Calvinist, and later a Lutheran. He was professor of Oriental languages at Königsberg.

SAADIA (882/892 – 942). Saadia Gaon, rabbi, philosopher, exegete who wrote extensively in Arabic.

SCHLICHTINGIUS, JONAS (1592-1661). Polish nobleman, this Socinian wrote commentaries on the New Testament.

SMALCIUS, VALENTINUS (1572-1622). German Socinian.

SOCINIANISM. Named for Italian theologian Fausto Sozzini (Lat: **Faustus Socinus**). It is nontrinitarian in its view of Christ and precursor to many forms of Unitarianism within Protestantism.

SOCINUS, (FAUSTUS 1539-1604). Fausto Paolo Sozzini. Italian theologian and founder of Socinianism, precursor to many forms of Unitarianism within Protestantism.

SPANHEIM, FREDRICK (1600-1649). Calvinist professor at Leiden.

STAUNTON, WILLIAM (17th-18th cent.). Clerk in Chancery, Socinian who denied the deity of Christ.

TARGUM. A Targum is a paraphrastic rendition of the Hebrew Scripture into Aramaic for Jews who did not speak Hebrew. They contain both oral tradition and interpretation of the Scripture and were probably first written down around the first century by the Jews.

TERTULLIAN (c. 155/160–225/250). Carthaginian apologist and polemicist who laid the foundations of Christology and Trinitarian Orthodoxy in the West, though he himself was later estranged from the catholic tradition.

THEODORET OF CYR (c. 393–466). Bishop of Cyr (Cyrrhus), he was an opponent of Cyril who commented extensively on Old Testament texts as a lucid exponent of Antiochene exegesis.

VATABLE, FRANÇOIS (d. 1547). French humanist scholar, a Hellenist, and a Hebraist.

WATERLAND, DANIEL (1683-1740), an English theologian who became Master of Magdalene College, Cambridge in 1714, Chancellor of the Diocese of York in 1722, and Archdeacon of Middlesex in 1730.

WHISTON, WILLIAM (1667-1752). English theologian, historian, and mathematician, a leading figure in the popularization of the ideas of Isaac Newton, including Newton's Arianism. Worked on important translations of the Antiquities of the Jews by Josephus.

Witsius, Herman (1636-1708). Dutch Calvinist who wrote an important work on the divine covenants.

ZANCHI, JEROME (1516-1590). Italian Protestant Reformer, very influential after Calvin's death.

Zohar (13th cent.). The foundational text of Kabbalah. It first appeared in Spain in the 13th century and was published by Moses de León who ascribed it to Shimon bar Yochai (Rashbi), a rabbi of the 2nd century.

Author Index

Scripture Index

ABOUT THE EDITOR

Doug has pastored the Reformed Baptist Church of Northern Colorado since 2001. He graduated from Bethel College in 1992, majoring in Marketing and minoring in Bible. He was a youth pastor for four years in Denver. He holds the Master of Divinity degree from Denver Seminary (2001).

Doug has served on councils and boards for two Baptist Associations, the current one which he helped found in 2016. The Reformed Baptist Network seeks to glorify God through fellowship and cooperation in fulfilling the Great Commission to the ends of the earth. There are currently 42 churches in this international association of churches.

Doug has co-hosted the radio show Journey's End, the Peeranormal podcast, started the Waters of Creation Publishing Company, owned two small business in Minneapolis, and has appeared on numerous podcasts and radio shows.

Married since 1994, he and Janelle are the proud parents of four beautiful young girls. Born and raised in Colorado, he has climbed all 54 of Colorado's 14,000 ft. mountains and also Mt. Rainier (WA) and Mt. Shasta (CA).

To find out more about any of these things go to:
https://www.dougvandorn.com/

The Church website is
https://rbcnc.com

Books in the Christ In All Scripture Series

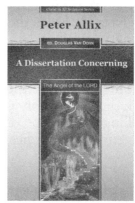

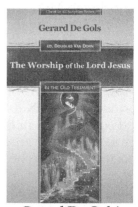

John Owen's treatment is perfect for those wanting to ground their theology of the Angel in the high orthodoxy of the Reformation. The quotations from the Fathers bolster his thesis.

Peter Allix's work is comprehensive and is especially helpful for those familiar with modern scholarship wishing to root their theology in conservative Protestant/Reformed orthodoxy.

Gerard De Gols' study, especially the second half, is imminently practical and would help anyone wanting to learn more about why it matters that Christ is present in the Old Testament.

Owen, Allix, and De Gols together in one volume, minus quotations from the Fathers and Reformers.

The Second Edition of *From the Shadows to the Savior*, it explores even more of the titles given to Christ in the OT than Allix goes into.

Practical sermons are for the further exploration of the fullness of Christ, especially as he is found in the NT.

Other Books by Doug Van Dorn

Giants: Sons of the Gods

The bestselling non-fiction book on Genesis 6 and the Nephilim.
150 reviews. 4.5+++ stars on Amazon.

Goliath. You know the story. But why is it in the Bible? Is it just to give us a little moral pick-me-up as we seek to emulate a small shepherd boy who defeated a giant? Have you ever wondered where Goliath came from? Did you know he had brothers, one with 24 fingers and toes? Did you know their ancestry is steeped in unimaginable horror? Genesis 6. The Nephilim. The first few verses of this chapter have long been the speculation of supernatural events that produced demigods and a flood that God used to destroy the whole world. The whole world remembers them. Once upon a time, all Christians knew them. But for many centuries this view was mocked, though it was the only known view at the time of the writing of the New Testament. Today, it is making a resurgence among Bible-believing scholars, and for good reason. The Nephilim were on the earth in those days, and also afterward...

This book delves deep into the dark and ancient recesses of our past to bring you rich treasures long buried. It is a carefully researched, heavily footnoted, and selectively illustrated story of the giants of the Bible. There is more here than meets the eye, much more. Here you will learn the invisible, supernatural storyline of the Bible that is always just beneath the surface, lurking like the spawn of the ancient leviathan. It is a storyline no person can afford to ignore any longer. Unlike other more sensational books on the topic, there is no undue speculation to be found here. The author is a Bible-believing Christian who refuses to use such ideas to tell you the end of the world is drawing nigh. Once you discover the truth about these fantastic creatures, you will come to see the ministry and work of Jesus Christ in a very new and exalting light. Come. Learn the fascinating, sobering, yet true story of real giants who played a significant role in the bible ... and still do so today.

Available in Paperback or Kindle at Amazon.com

The Unseen Realm: Q & A Companion
Edited by Michael Heiser.
Published by Lexham Press.

In *The Unseen Realm*, Dr. Michael S. Heiser unpacked 15 years of research while exploring what the Bible really says about the supernatural world. That book has nearly 900 reviews and a five-star rating. It is a game-changer

Doug helps you further explore *The Unseen Realm* with a fresh perspective and an easy-to-follow format. The book summarizes key concepts and themes from Heiser's book and includes questions aimed at helping you gain a deeper understanding of the biblical author's supernatural worldview.

The format is that of a catechism: A Question followed by the Answer. There are 95 Questions (nod to Martin Luther) divided into 12 Parts:

Part I—God
Part II—The Lesser Gods
Part III—The Sons of God
Part IV—Divine Council
Part V—Sin, Rebellion, and the Fall
Part VI—Rebellion before the flood
Part VII—Rebellion after the flood
Part VIII—The Promise Anticipated
Part IX—The Promise Fulfilled
Part X—The Good News

Available in Paperback or Kindle at Amazon.com or on the Bible-software platform Logos at Logos.com

From the Shadows to the Savior:
Christ in the Old Testament

Few subjects are as important--yet ignored or misapplied--as the one addressed in this book. Jesus Christ is the absolute center and focus of the totality of God's word. Many people confess this belief, since Jesus himself taught it (Luke 24:27; John 5:39). Christians have done well to see this on one or two levels, yet truly understanding just how primary he is as an actor—even in the Old Testament—is something few have considered.

In this book, adapted from a series of blog posts for the Decablog, Doug helps us see the light of Christ that emerges from the dark hallways of Scriptures that so many find outdated, unintelligible, and irrelevant for today's Church.

Learn how Christ is found in such things as prophecy, typology, and the law. Then, come in for a deeper study of how the Person himself is actually present, walking, speaking, and acting, beginning in the very first book of the Bible. Learn how words such as "Word," "Name," "Glory," and "Wisdom" are all ideas that the Scripture itself attaches to Christ who in the OT is called The Angel of the LORD. Then see if such ideas don't radically change the way you think about all of God's word in this truly life-changing summary of Christ in the Old Testament.

Chapters:
NT Passages and Reflections
Christ in Prophecy
Christ in Typology
Christ and the Law
Christ: The Angel of the LORD
Christ: The Word of God
Christ: The Name of the LORD
Christ: The Wisdom of God
Christ: The Son of God
Christ: The Glory of God
Christ: The Right Arm of God

Available in Paperback or Kindle at Amazon.com

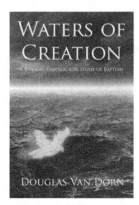

Waters of Creation:
A Biblical-Theological Study of Baptism

This is the one book on baptism that you must read. It was seven years in the making. Doug believes that until a new approach is taken, separations over the meaning, mode, and recipients of baptism will never be bridged.

This new approach traces the roots of baptism deep into the OT Scriptures. When understood properly, we discover that baptism is always the sign that God has used to initiate his people into a new creation. Baptism in the NT is not "new." Rather, it derives its origin from OT predecessors. It has a direct, sacramental counterpart, and it isn't circumcision. It is baptism. When we understand that baptism comes from baptism, especially in its sacramental expression in the priestly covenant, reasons for the NT practice begin to make perfect sense.

Now Baptists have an argument that infant Baptists can finally understand, because we are beginning our argument in the same place. This is an Old Testament covenantal approach to the Baptist position with baptistic conclusions as to the mode and recipients of baptism. That's what happens when we root baptism in baptism rather than circumcision.

Chapters:
The Baptism of Jesus
Baptism and the Sanctuary
Baptism and the Priesthood
Baptism and the Covenant
Implications for Christian Baptism

Available in Paperback or Kindle at Amazon.com

Covenant Theology:
A Reformed Baptist Primer

Douglas Van Dorn

Covenant theology is often said to be the domain of infant Baptists alone. But there really are such things as Reformed Baptists who believe in covenant theology as a basic system for approaching Scripture.

This primer sets out to give the basics of a Reformed Baptist covenant theology and to do so in a way that is understandable to the uninitiated. It was originally a series we did on Sunday nights at our church. It agrees with classical formulations of covenant theology in that there is a Covenant of Redemption, a Covenant of Works, and a Covenant of Grace in the Bible.

The book takes a multi-perspective approach to the Covenant of Redemption in that this covenant is the basis for the classic formula that Christ's death is sufficient for all, but efficient for the elect. It sees the Covenant of Works for Adam in a broader context of a covenant made with all of creation, a covenant where laws establish the parameters for creation's existence.

It differs from Paedobaptist covenant theology in that it sees the Covenant of Grace as only properly coming through Jesus Christ. OT gracious covenants are typological of the Covenant of Grace but save people on the basis of the coming work of Christ through faith alone. This is the traditional way Reformed Baptists have articulated the Covenant of Grace.

Finally, it sees an entire covenant in the Old Testament as often (but not always) missing from formulations of covenant theology. In the opinion of the author, this "priestly covenant" is vital to a proper understanding of 1. The continuity of the practice of baptism from OT to NT, 2. The answer to why we never find infants being baptized in the NT, and 3. A more precise way to parse the legal aspects of the OT economy, thereby helping us understand why the moral law continues today. This volume works from the basic presupposition that continuity in God's word is more basic than discontinuity. In this, it differs from dispensationalism and new covenant theology. The book suggests that this is the greatest strength of covenant theology, which does also recognize discontinuity.

Available in Paperback or Kindle at Amazon.com

Galatians:
A Supernatural Justification

A play on words, the subtitle of this book gives you the two main points it tries to get across. Galatians central message teaches how a person is *justified* before a holy God. This once precious and central teaching of Protestant theology is often misunderstood or relegated the pile of irrelevant, stale doctrine.

Perhaps that is why the Apostle Paul supercharges his teaching with an oft-overlooked side of this letter - the *supernatural* beings who tempt us and teach us to give up the only truth that will save us. Galatian Christians would have been familiar with these supernatural beings; their culture was steeped in it. Thus, they mistake Paul for the messenger-healer god Hermes, and Barnabas for Zeus. Paul's warning: "Even if we or an angel from heaven should preach to you a gospel contrary to the one we preached to you, let him be accursed." This is Paul's fatherly way of showing his children in the faith that the gospel is paramount; it alone is able to save. Such a warning like this can have new power, as people are returning with reckless abandon to the worship of the old gods.

This book is from a series of sermons preached at the Reformed Baptist Church of Northern Colorado in 2011.

Available in Paperback or Kindle at Amazon.com

The Five Solas
of the Reformation

The 500th anniversary of the Reformation occurred in 2017. It was October 31, 1517 that Martin Luther nailed his 95 Thesis to the door of the great cathedral at Wittenberg, Germany. He had no idea what that simple act would do. His bold proclamation and challenge to for Rome to reform her ways and beliefs was met with hostility from some and great sympathy from others. Out of this sympathy arose Protestantism, a movement deeply concerned with grounding all things on Holy Scripture, giving glory to God alone, and recovering for that generation the biblical gospel of Jesus Christ. In five chapters, Doug Van Dorn takes us back to these ancient catchphrases that once moved a continent. Scripture Alone, Grace Alone, Faith Alone, Christ Alone, and To God Be the Glory Alone became the rallying cry of all who longed to see men and women, boys and girls saved and set free from sin, death, and the devil. The end of the book contains four helpful Appendices on songs, Church Fathers on the solas, a bibliography for further research, and a letter from Martin Luther.

Available in Paperback or Kindle at Amazon.com